A Source Book of
Trams

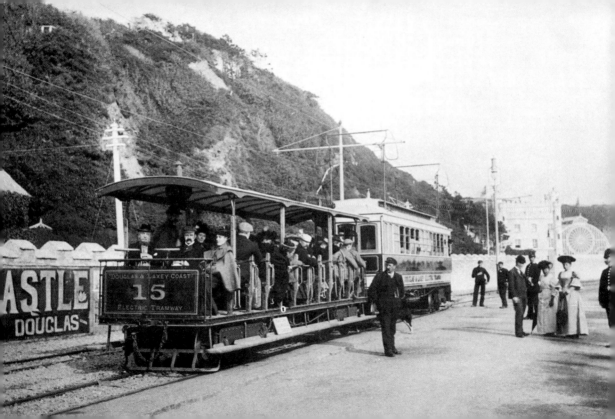

A Source Book of
Trams

J. H. Price

First published in Great Britain in 1980 by Ward Lock Limited

This edition published in 2008 by Bounty Books,
a division of Octopus Publishing Group Ltd
2–4 Heron Quays, London E14 4JP
www.octopusbooks.co.uk

An Hachette Livre UK Company
www.hachettelivre.co.uk

ISBN: 978-0-753717-83-7

A CIP catalogue record for this book is available from the British Library

Printed and bound in China

Contents

Introduction

For about half a century, from the 1880s to the 1930s, street railways (tramways) were the principal form of public transport in towns. Some countries use them today; others have changed to buses, trolleybuses, or underground railways. There are few trams in Britain today outside museums, so parts of this book are in the past tense, but some of the preserved examples give rides to visitors during the summer months.

Trams were distinctively individual vehicles, rarely mass-produced. In Britain, nearly every town had its own style. Street scenes of the tramway period are identified by the rails in the carriageway, and the expert can identify and locate almost any street scene, if a tram is featured. The tram was usually double-ended, with driving controls at each end. It had no steering gear, for being on rails it steered itself. At the terminus, the driver and conductor just changed places for the return trip. Most British trams were double-deck, and many lasted in service for thirty or forty years.

HRH Prince Richard, Duke of Gloucester, tries his hand at driving Blackpool toastrack 166 at the Tramway Museum, Crich, on 9 June 1976. The left-hand tram (1297) is from Glasgow.

Trams had flanged steel or iron wheels that ran in grooved rails in the road surface. Most British trams were rather noisy; steel tyres on steel rails usually are. Modern trams abroad have rubber-resilient wheels and silent-running gears, and are quieter than buses. The rails in Britain were usually 1435 mm (4 ft 8½ in) apart, as on the railways, but there were narrow-gauge tramways with 1067 mm (3 ft 6 in) gauge tracks, and some odd gauges like 1219 mm (4 ft) and 1416 mm (4 ft 7¾ in). On the European Continent, the most popular tramway track gauge after 1435 mm is 1000 mm (3 ft 3⅜ in), especially in Switzerland. Some tramways in Britain were legally light railways, built under different legislation.

This book is about the vehicle rather than the track, but there were so many designs that it is not possible to include every type, or every user. Those selected are typical examples, chosen to portray stages in vehicle development rather than geographical coverage. These stages were defined some years ago by a committee of transport historians reporting to the Museum of British Transport, which the writer chaired. Its findings remained unpublished, and it is pleasing to have this opportunity

to place them on record. The author here acknowledges the participation and contribution of his fellow committee-members (especially G. B. Claydon, R. Elliott and Charles E. Lee) and those of his correspondents who helped with the original paper.

The story of most British tramways now belongs to industrial archaeology, and forms an active and popular branch of museum activity. But there is nothing outdated in the idea of electric vehicles on rails; they have a greater development potential than the motor bus, and are still the main form of city transport in many countries. Modern tramways, known today as Light Rapid Transit, can offer social and environmental benefits that can justify the high cost of track and cars. It was these costs that brought about the near-demise of the tram in Britain, where city transport was expected to pay its way and only low-cost systems could be used. The changeover from trams to buses in Britain was merely a short-term solution to a long-term problem.

However, the tram in Britain is not yet extinct. Blackpool has its busy 17·7 km (11 mile) coastal tramway, horse trams still ply along Douglas promenade in the Isle of Man, taking passengers to a scenic interurban tramway, the Manx Electric to Laxey and Ramsey with its mountain branch to Snaefell Summit. Britain's one cable tramway, a street funicular, takes tourists from Llandudno up to the Great Orme, and Volks Railway at Brighton (a tramway in all but name) still links the Aquarium with Black Rock and the new Marina. At Seaton, Devon, half-size replica trams on 838 mm (2 ft 9 in) gauge track provide a tourist service to two nearby villages, and preserved trams are at work on museum lines at Crich (Derbyshire), Beamish (County Durham), Carlton Colville (Lowestoft) and in Heaton Park at Manchester. Modern Continental trams formed the design basis for the articulated Metrocars of the new Tyne & Wear Metro at Newcastle, adapted in this instance to work on railway tracks. And if the oil runs out, the tram and the trolleybus with their reliance on electricity will be needed again to provide transport in our cities.

The contents of this book are divided into three parts. Part One covers the development of the tramway as a form of passenger locomotion from the 1850s to the time about eighty years later when it no longer enjoyed a near-monopoly in urban transport. Part Two continues the British story to the present day and takes a brief look abroad, and Part Three is a brief survey of the technical aspects.

London, July 1952.

Glossary

Most tramway terms were shared with electrical, railway, cabinet-making or engineering terminology. Below are some examples of terms and words with special tramway meanings.

Balcony car – covered double-decker with roofed open-end sections upstairs.

Bellamy-roof car – covered double-decker with unroofed open-end sections upstairs.

Bow collector – uni-directional sprung sliding current collector.

Brake staff – vertical spindle on the driver's platform with ratchet handle and base, operating the wheel brakes through chains and levers.

Bulkhead – partition extending across the car with a central door leading into the saloon.

Canopy – semi-circular extension of lower deck roof over car platform.

Canopy switch – main switch, usually mounted on the canopy ceiling.

Combination car – single-decker with both a closed saloon and some open bench seats.

Conduit system – conductor rails in a subterranean tube with access through a continuous slot.

Controller – enclosed cylindrical drum with copper segments and fingers used to regulate the speed of the car by varying the voltage fed to the motors.

Cross-bench car – car with full width transverse benches, leaving no gangway.

Dash – semi-circular panel extending round the car platform to waist level.

Decency boards – panels enclosing a tram's upper deck and intended to screen the legs of passengers.

Demi-car – small purpose-built one-man tram.

Direct stairs – stairs rising in an anti-clockwise half-turn or quarter-turn from the platform.

Dry seat – turnover seat for open cars, providing a dry surface after rain.

Feeder box – roadside cabinet with switchgear feeding current to the overhead line.

Fixed head trolley – trolley head in line with pole, unable to swivel independently.

Frog – junction of two trolley wires, usually with a movable tongue.

Garden seat – seat (usually with reversible backrest) on which passengers face the direction of travel.

Grand Union – right-angled intersection of two double tracks with double-track connections around all four corners.

Interurban – tramway built to provide transport between separate towns.

Knifeboard – bench seats arranged back-to-back along the car centre line.

Magnetic brake – spring-mounted brake shoes which cling to the rails when magnetized electrically.

Maximum traction – bogie truck with one large pair and one small pair of wheels.

Monitor – roof structure with raised centre. The lower sides conceal ventilating spaces.

Motorman – tram driver.

PCC car – car built under the patents of the Transit Research Corporation set up by the Presidents' Conference Committee of American tramways.

Pendulum truck – truck in which the axles can move laterally independently of the frame and adapt themselves to irregularities in the track.

Plough – current collector used with the conduit system.

Point iron – iron bar used to turn points by hand.

Point turner – electrical route-selecting device at junctions.

Radial truck – truck in which the axles can adjust themselves to track curvature.

Rail grinder – car or machine with carborundum blocks to erase rail corrugations.

Reserved track – track laid elsewhere than in the public road.

Resilient wheel – wheel containing a rubber sandwich between tyre and centre plate.

Reversed stairs – stairs rising in a clockwise spiral from the platform.

Reversing key – controller spindle used to reverse the flow of current through the motor field coils.

Rheostatic brake – electric brake in which the car's momentum produces electrical energy which is then dissipated as heat in the resistances.

Rocker panel – the lower side panel of a car with waisted side construction.

Rosette – wall mounting serving to anchor a span wire to a building.

Sand pedal – foot pedal releasing dry sand from hoppers on to the rails to improve adhesion.

Slipper brake – shoes which the driver can press down on to the rails by operating a handwheel.

Surface contact – a series of metal studs in the road from which the car collects current through a magnetized contact skate.

Swivel trolley – trolley head free to pivot in relation to the trolley pole.

Toastrack – roofless cross-bench car.

Trolley – trolley pole, head, wheel and base.

Trolley head – mounting for trolley wheel or skid.

Trolley pole – spring-loaded arm on swivel base, arranged to press the trolley wheel or skid to the underside of the overhead wire.

Trolley retriever – spring-loaded drum to keep the trolley rope taut and wind it in in the event of a sudden jerking force such as a dewirement.

Trolley reverser – triangle of overhead wires with spring-loaded frogs on which the trolley will reverse and re-emerge automatically when the car changes direction.

Trolley standard – vertical pillar containing the springs, hinge and swivel mounting for the trolley pole.

Trolley wheel – grooved pulley arranged to run along the underside of the overhead wire.

Truck – self-contained rectangular frame for the wheels, axles and motors, detachable from the car. Four wheel trams have single trucks, eight wheel cars have bogie trucks (or bogies).

Tumblehome – contraction in width of a tramcar below the waist.

Waist panel – the upper side panel of a car with waisted side construction.

Works car – non-passenger tramcar used for stores transport, track cleaning, etc.

**PART ONE
HISTORICAL**

The Horse Tram

Tramways are older than railways. The word was in use in the seventeenth and eighteenth centuries to describe early wagonways with wooden beams or granite blocks, later with iron plates, along which horses drew wagons from a mine or quarry to a wharf. These mineral tramways evolved into railways, and do not form part of this book.

In the mid-nineteenth century the tramway became a street railway, used to provide passenger transport in towns, where a span of horses could haul a much greater load on rails than on the rough road surfaces of the day. The first example, the New York & Harlaem line of 1832, began with 3-compartment vehicles resembling early railway carriages, and when the idea began to spread in the 1850s, the vehicles at first resembled a horse omnibus placed on rails, the passengers entering and leaving by the rear and passing their money up through a hatch to the driver on his box. Tramcars of this type appeared in Paris and the USA, and are thought to have been used on the tramway service operated by W. J. Curtis along the dockside railway in Liverpool from March 1859 to January 1860. The type of vehicle is known from a patent drawing of 1856 submitted by Curtis, and resembled the cars in use on the pioneer 1855 tramway in Paris.

In 1858, Andrew Palles of Philadelphia introduced an improved vehicle more suited to the new medium, and this type of car soon established itself wherever tramways began to take root. The car was double-ended, which avoided the need for special turning arrangements; instead of using shafts, the horses or mules were harnessed to the car by a splinter-bar, with a pin which was lifted out at the terminus, horses and bar being walked around to the other end and re-attached. Instead of being seated aloft, the driver now stood to his task on a large open platform at floor level, with a vertical brake-handle at his right hand, which through chains, rods and levers acted on all four wheels, no matter from which end it was applied. Adhesion was assisted by sand, kept in a box on the platform, which the driver would scatter on the road in front to reduce the slipping of the horses' hoofs. The driver's left hand held the reins, but the car was steered by its flanged wheels and the rails.

The platform was cantilevered out from the main frame, and provided an easy and convenient entrance with access at the sides instead of the rear. A dashboard was fitted to each platform to protect the driver and the front end of the car body from mud thrown up by the horses. The bulkhead at each end had a sliding door and the window sashes were raised to open and had fixed top-lights with gothic or semi-circular heads and ornamental ground glass. Strap hangers for standing passengers also appeared. The wheels were of chilled cast iron, with a diameter of about 762 mm (30 in), attached to the axles as in railway practice. The projecting journals revolved in axleboxes, which in turn supported the car body through rubber mountings.

Cars of this type were used on the first British tramway to be built as such, George Francis Train's line at Birkenhead (opened on 30 August 1860). Some of the cars were single-deck, but the superiority of railed motion permitted the installation of additional seats on the roof, and this practice was adopted for two of Train's 1860 cars at Birkenhead, one of which is shown at the inauguration. These had a back-to-back 'knifeboard' seat along the roof, with access by a steep iron ladder at each end. A turtle-back roof form was adopted to bring the weight of the top seats and passengers squarely on to the body pillars without exerting side-thrust.

BIRKENHEAD PARK & WOODSIDE-FERRY

Britain's first street tramway; a car of George Francis Train's line at Birkenhead on the opening day, 30 August 1860.

G. F. Train also built tramways in 1860–1 in London, Darlington and the Potteries, but the London and Darlington lines were short-lived.

G. F. Train's first cars were imported from America, but his manager, George Starbuck, soon set up a tramcar manufactory at Cleveland Street, Birkenhead (the first outside the USA), which supplied almost all British tramways until the mid-1870s and also built many cars for customers on the Continent and overseas. Starbuck's cars generally followed the 1860 design, save for the later use of metal springs instead of rubber blocks. An 1869 Starbuck double-decker is preserved in Brussels, and an 1873 single-decker from Oporto is at the Tramway Museum, Crich. Starbuck running gear was used in building the oldest surviving British tramcar, a Ryde Pier car of 1871 in the Hull Transport Museum. The Birkenhead works were taken over in 1886 by George F. Milnes, Starbuck's secretary, but competition and over-expansion brought the enterprise to an end in 1904.

In the 1870s, George Starbuck turned to a more simple design of horse car, cheaper and lighter than the 1860 type. This saving of weight allowed a greater carrying capacity for the same horsepower, while single-deck one-horse cars became practicable for light traffic. An example is Sheffield horse

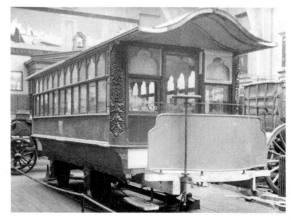

Britain's oldest surviving tramcar was built in 1871 for the Ryde Pier tramway. Originally horse-drawn, it became a trailer when the pier tramway was electrified. Since 1936 it has been in the Hull Transport Museum.

Sheffield horse car 15 of 1874 during the city's 1961 Christmas Shopping Festival.

car 15 of 1874 in the Tramway Museum at Crich, shown here running in Sheffield during the Christmas Shopping Festival in December 1961. Toplights were discarded, and these less ornate cars usually had fixed instead of opening windows, ventilation now being provided by a short row of small glazed ventilators in each side of the turtle-back roof. The straight or spiral iron ladder of the early double-deck cars gave way to a more convenient quarter-turn iron stairway, and the cars were lit at night by an oil lamp at each end, mounted in the 'lantern panel' of the bulkhead.

For a time in the 1870s, the demand for cars exceeded the supply, and the various London horse tramways imported many cars from the builder John Stephenson & Co. of New York. The demand led several railway carriage and wagon builders to enter the tramway field, and horse cars were soon being built by the Gloucester Railway Carriage & Wagon Co., the Lancaster Wagon Co., the Ashbury Carriage & Iron Co., the Midland Railway Carriage & Wagon Co., and by the Metropolitan Railway Carriage & Wagon Co. of Saltley, Birmingham. The chief designer of the Ashbury company, John Eades, devised and introduced the 'Eades Patent Reversible' car, of which the body could rotate on a turntable to save the work of unhitching the horses at the terminus, and which also eliminated the weight of the second platform and stairs. A demonstration model built by the original manufacturer survives in the collection of the Manchester Transport Museum Society.

In many parts of the world, extensive use was made of open horse trams fitted with full-width cross-benches, but the British climate restricted these to summer use, mainly at seaside resorts. Some had fixed back-to-back seats, but most had benches with reversible backs. Those without roofs soon attracted to themselves the name 'toastrack', by reason of their resemblance to the familiar breakfast-table utensil, and this term was sometimes applied without distinction to all cross-bench cars whether roofed or open. Both varieties can still be seen in use each summer at Douglas, Isle of Man, together with some closed single-deck horse cars, on what is now the last traditional horse tramway in Europe. The Douglas cars have several modern features such as spring traces and roller bearings, but have conserved their traditional form. They also have battery lighting.

A maker's demonstration model of the Eades Patent Reversible horse car, built to show how the body could be rotated at a terminus to avoid unhitching the horses.

Horse trams still run every summer along the promenade at Douglas, Isle of Man. This one was built in 1902.

The general layout and design of the single-deck horse tram underwent little further change, but the late 1880s saw gradual improvements to the double-decker. 'Decency boards' intended to shield the legs of upper deck passengers were fitted to screen the upper deck, stairs were more commodious, and from 1886 the back-to-back knifeboard seat fitted astride the turtle-back roof gradually yielded pride of place to the garden seat in which the top deck passenger faced the direction of travel. This feature had first appeared in 1881 on London horse buses, but its extension to trams involved the use of a reversible backrest, one of the most distinctive and unforgettable features of the British tramcar. This top deck layout required a full-width floor, slightly cambered for drainage, and the addition of this floor above the previous roof and ventilators resulted in a complicated roof-structure by which fresh air would enter concealed spaces from outside and could then be admitted to the saloon by opening a row of patterned glass half-lights. This became known as a monitor roof.

A final development in the horse tramcar from 1894 onwards was the provision of fewer and larger windows. After this date few horse cars were built, and the rapid development of the electric tramway meant that many existing horse cars enjoyed only a

A former Cardiff garden-seat horse tram that became a trailer car in electric service at Guernsey.

short life. Some were converted into electric cars (an example of 1891, converted in 1904, has been preserved at Portsmouth) and others were used as trailers, but the majority were sold for other uses. The advanced stage which the techniques of timber-selection and body construction had reached by the end of the horse tram era is shown by the fact that occasional specimens can still be found doing duty as storehouses and potting sheds.

The Steam Tram

The already long-established use of steam traction on railways soon brought attempts to mechanize the horse tramway by the same means. In 1861, G. F. Train had registered in Britain a Grice and Long patent for working tramways by steam, but this and other similar schemes were for years frustrated by the provisions of the Locomotives Act, 1865, which limited mechanically-propelled road vehicles to 3 km/h (2 mph) in towns and 6 km/h (4 mph) elsewhere, with a man to walk in front (until 1878 he had also to carry a red flag). These conditions were not relaxed until 1896, but after the practicability of steam traction had been demonstrated in 1876–7 on the Wantage, Swansea & Mumbles and Vale of Clyde tramways (which possessed local statutory authority) Parliament in 1879 sanctioned the use of mechanical power on tramways, subject to Board of Trade inspection and regulation but exempt from the Act of 1865. It was thus the steam tram which first won the freedom of Britain's roads for mechanical traction.

The first steam trams to be tried in the British Isles took the form of a combined engine and car. The first such vehicle, designed by John Grantham, was demonstrated in London in 1873 and ran on the Wantage Tramway from 1876 to 1887. Other examples were tried at Sheffield, Dublin and Portsmouth, but without lasting results, though self-propelled steam cars designed by Rowan, Purrey, Komarek and Serpollet were used up to about 1914 on the Continent. The disadvantages of the self-propelled steam car included heat, noise, vibration, unsuitable weight distribution, difficulty of access for maintenance, and the fact that the whole vehicle had to be taken out of service if the engine broke down. The public were, moreover, more familiar with the use of separate locomotives on railways, and after the first experiments the self-propelled steam car gave way in Britain to the separate engine and car.

Steam trams were in general use in the towns of the West Midlands and the North of England from about 1881 to 1901, with a few systems elsewhere in the British Isles. The regulations governing steam tramway operation drawn up by the Board of Trade in 1875 on the recommendations of Major-General C. S. Hutchinson, were very stringent. They required that engines should not emit steam or smoke, that they should be free from noise, that all fire should be concealed from view, and that all machinery should be concealed from view above 102 mm (4 in) from rail level. In addition, the engine had to be equipped

The first steam tram to be tried in Britain; John Grantham's self-propelled car of 1873, reproduced from *The Engineer*. It was later used on the Wantage Tramway.

with a governor to ensure that a speed of 13 km/h (8 mph) was not exceeded. The regulation concerning smoke and steam was especially harsh, involving many lawsuits, and in 1884 it was relaxed to permit the emission of smoke or steam provided that the amounts concerned did not constitute reasonable grounds for complaint on the part of public or passengers. In later years it was common for some of the regulations to be more honoured in the breach than in the observance.

These regulations, together with the layout of the tramways which restricted the width of the engines and sometimes the chimney height, and which usually required that the engines should be capable of being driven from either end, meant therefore that the construction of a tramway locomotive needed more detailed consideration than a railway engine. Few of the well-known firms engaged in building railway locomotives ventured into the tramway field; the most notable to do so were Kitson & Co. of Leeds, Black, Hawthorn & Co. of Gateshead, and Beyer, Peacock & Co. of Manchester. Other specialists in this field were Merryweather & Sons of London, who as fire engine manufacturers had experience in building light steam pumping engines, Thomas Green & Son of Leeds, and the Falcon Works of Loughborough, whose founder, Henry

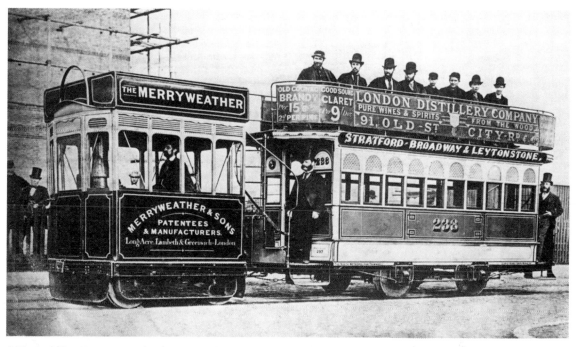

A Merryweather steam tram engine demonstrated on the North Metropolitan Tramways in 1880, hauling a horse car with the early form of iron ladder.

Hughes, did much pioneer work. A few engines were also made by Dick, Kerr & Co. of Kilmarnock.

The 700 or so steam engines built for British tramways were almost all of the 0–4–0 wheel arrangement, the wheels being coupled as in railway practice. The cylinders were mounted high to avoid dust and mud and, to meet the Board of Trade requirements, the engines were coke fired and fitted with air or water cooled condensers on the roof, or with exhaust superheaters to consume the smoke or render it invisible. Except for the very successful vertical-boilered locomotives built during the 1880s to the design of William Wilkinson of Wigan, the superiority of the horizontal boiler soon manifested itself and most locomotives were of this pattern. The engines had enclosed sides and ends, to comply with the regulations, so the working conditions of the driver compared favourably with his counterparts on horse and early electric trams. There was no separate fireman.

The speed governor was usually worked off the driving axle, but on some later engines it was operated by a fifth wheel. Most engines also had a speed indicator, while the driver's whistle, which was the only audible warning on horse trams, was replaced by a bell. Locomotive braking was by means of brake blocks applied to the wheels by hand linkage and by steam acting through brake cylinders. The governor generally actuated the steam brake. Sand hoppers on the locomotive applied sand direct to the rails through pipes to assist adhesion in bad conditions. Oil headlamps were carried on the roofs, and a red lamp was placed at the rear when running light.

Britain's urban steam tramways were all later electrified, the last being Rawtenstall in 1909, but a few rural steam tramways continued to carry passengers until the 1920s. Rural steam tramways were in widespread use on the Continent, particularly in Belgium, the Netherlands, and Northern Italy, those in Belgium forming a nationwide network which remained almost intact until the early 1950s, though by then worked mainly by diesel railcars. Four British steam tram engines survive in museums, one each at Hull, Belfast, Crich and Dinting; the Crich tram engine, a Wilkinson-type vertical-boilered engine built by Beyer, Peacock & Co., was built in 1885 for service in New South Wales, but returned to Britain in 1890 and served for many years as shunter at Beyer, Peacock's works. Steam tram engines can be seen at work each summer on preserved lines at Hoorn in Holland and Erezée in Belgium.

The passenger trailers used by the majority of steam tram operators were double-deckers. Initially,

Steam trams lasted much longer in Belgium than in Britain. The author found this one working in Antwerp in 1947.

these were 4-wheel horse cars adapted or copied for steam haulage and used singly or occasionally in pairs. Some tramway undertakings (for example Bradford, Birmingham & Aston, and Huddersfield) experimented with single-ended cars of the Eades reversible type (manually rotated) since these while incorporating a glazed screen at the front end avoided the necessity for a turning circle or triangle at each terminus.

After the first few years, the Board of Trade ruled that on urban steam tramways each engine should draw only one car, and to make full use of the tractive power available a much larger car about 9 m (30 ft) long was introduced, mounted on bogies. This required the use of a rolled steel underframe with truss rods, as in later railway carriage practice, the frame being continued through to the platforms, and the bogies being placed at the extreme ends of the car to ensure stability. The leading bogie was generally coupled direct to the engine by means of a draw bar and chain, but after 1890 the chain could be dispensed with if the drawgear was by means of a screw coupling. The bogies were of plate frame type, and the wheels were of chilled iron.

The proximity of the bogies to the ends of the car caused the entrances to the platforms to be displaced to the corners, and a gate was often placed across the entrance not in use. The lower saloon retained the longitudinal wooden seating of horse car practice and the complicated double-deck roof structure was also perpetuated. At first, the cars had open top decks, but, despite the regulations, fumes and smuts were emitted by the engines to the discomfort of the upper deck passengers. One or two tramways retained the open top decks and charged outside passengers a lower fare, but the majority sought to protect them from the nuisance by a solid or glazed vertical screen at each end. Later, a simple roof of low headroom was added, supported by the end screens and by side stanchions, and this evolved by stages into a completely enclosed top deck, the forerunner of the top-covered double-deck passenger vehicles used today. Top-deck seating followed the same pattern as that of the horse car, with knifeboard seating down to 1886 and a gradual change to garden seats thereafter.

Car lighting was initially by an oil lantern in a panel at each end of the lower saloon, and by two similar lamps (where provided) upstairs. Gas lighting and

A Merryweather steam tram engine at work on the North London Suburban Tramways in 1885. This steam tramway, unlike most, had only open-top cars.

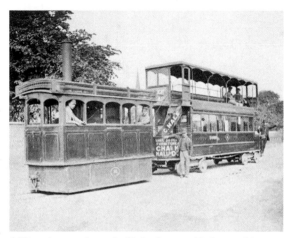

A Kitson tram-engine and a Starbuck covered trailer used from 1885 between Dudley and Wolverhampton.

acetylene lighting were sometimes adopted in later days. Communication between car and engine was by means of a bell cord on the lower deck actuating either a gong on the front platform of the car or a gong on the locomotive. The conductor used a whistle when on the upper deck. It was usual for the car to be braked from the locomotive, either mechanically or (more rarely) by a vacuum brake. In either case, the car brake would be applied automatically in the event of a coupling failure. The car was equipped with a hand brake, and on steeply graded systems, it became compulsory also to have slipper brakes, consisting of wooden track shoes, two to each bogie, which the conductor applied from a wheel on the platform.

Steam tramway trailer cars were built by the same firms already mentioned as horse car builders. No full-size steam tramway trailer has been preserved in any British transport museum, but there are plans to renovate the body of a Dundee car which survived for many years as an anglers' shelter alongside a reservoir, for ultimate inclusion in the collection at Crich.

The final form of the British steam tram. A Wilkinson-type engine and enclosed double-deck car at Blackburn in 1900.

The Cable Tram

The principle of rope haulage by stationary winding engine was frequently used in the early days of railways, and rope traction is still employed for working steep inclines on mineral lines and for funicular railways, generally known in Britain as cliff lifts. The idea was first applied to street tramways in 1873 in San Francisco by A. S. Hallidie, a British subject born in London in 1836. Hallidie's system employed a cable running continuously in a conduit below the track, which could be picked up or released by a gripper with soft metal jaws suspended from the car body and passing through a slot in the road to reach the cable. The mechanism was mounted in a small 4-wheeled gripper car in which the driver rode, and from which he could apply a powerful mechanical track brake to hold the car at the stops when he released the cable. A few passengers could ride on the gripper car, but the remainder travelled in a 4-wheeled trailer of normal horse car design.

The success of this pioneer line brought the widespread adoption of cable tramways for steeply graded routes, and occasionally also for complete tramway systems such as those at Chicago, Melbourne (Australia) and Edinburgh. Hallidie's system was adopted on six British tramways, commencing

A cable 'dummy' and trailer operated by the London Tramways Company on the Brixton service in the 1890s. The cars were hauled by horses north of Kennington.

Cable cars still run in San Francisco, the city that was their birthplace.

with the Highgate Hill tramway in London in 1884; the others, in order of opening, were Edinburgh, Birmingham, Brixton Hill, Matlock and Douglas. The early San Francisco lines had used separate gripper cars and trailers because of the abrupt changes of gradient at intersecting streets, and this pattern of operation was copied unnecessarily elsewhere.

The Highgate Hill line began with 4-wheel gripper cars and trailers, but soon introduced the self-contained cable car with its own gripper at either end, the rear one being withdrawn when not in use. Similar bogie cars were used from the start on the other British cable tramways, except for the Brixton Hill line in South London, which kept to the separate gripper car so that the trailers could be hauled onward by horses to the London termini. Some of these cars were fitted with their own detachable grippers in 1899, and in 1903 similar equipment was fitted experimentally to some electric cars, but these proved too heavy for the cables. In Edinburgh, the front and rear grippers could be used in conjunction with each other, whatever the direction of travel.

Apart from the gripper gear, the body construction of cable cars resembled that of horse cars or steam tram trailers. Most had open top decks; the only top-covered examples were at Edinburgh, from 1907. Some Edinburgh cars had reversed stairs, rising clockwise from the platform. The cable cars at Douglas (Isle of Man) were single-deck, and included some open cars, though these were of cross-bench type with the grippers and bogies at each end, and not of the distinctive San Francisco type with the gripper flanked by longitudinal seats. Certain other British cable trams had interior transverse seating, on account of the steep gradients. Cable cars were fitted with fenders, lifeguards and warning bells. The lighting was usually by oil lamps, but gas and battery lighting were used on some systems in later years.

The jaws of the gripper were operated by either a wheel or a lever device. Wheel brakes were fitted to both dummies and carriages, and those on steeply graded lines also had slipper brakes. This feature, the application of brake shoes directly to the rails (later to become common on British electric tramways) was introduced to tramways by cable operators. A separate emergency brake was sometimes fitted to grip the slot rails, and the Matlock cars were fitted with chocks. The cable itself was used to retard the cars, since they were not normally permitted to release the cable when proceeding downhill, and the speed of the cable was governed at the engine house. To assist braking, sand hoppers were placed on the cars, either on the platforms or in the lower saloons under the end seats.

Interior view of a Matlock cable tram of 1893, showing the gripper control wheel. The transverse seating, adopted on account of the steep gradient, antedated by many years the general adoption of transverse seats in electric trams.

Britain's steepest cable tramway was at Matlock, with a maximum gradient of 1 in 5½. It ran from 1893 to 1927.

Four of Britain's cable tramways were later electrified (the last, Edinburgh, in 1920–3) and the other two closed in 1927 and 1929. The Glasgow Subway was cable-worked until 1935, using an enlarged type of detachable gripper. Two cross-bench Douglas cable cars which survived since 1929 as the frame for a Manx bungalow were recovered some years ago and used to re-create one of the cars, now displayed in the horse car depot at Douglas. Edinburgh Corporation have preserved a short section of cable track in Waterloo Place, and also possess a fine model of a cable car.

The principle of tramway traction by means of a cable in a conduit can still be seen on the lower part of the Great Orme Tramway at Llandudno, which although using cars of conventional tramway form is worked as a street funicular, controlled from a winding house. Trolley poles and an overhead wire are provided for signalling and telephone purposes. A similar but much shorter line once operated in Swansea. Most cable cars were built by the established tramcar builders such as Milnes, Falcon and Metropolitan, often to the order of Dick, Kerr & Co. of Kilmarnock who equipped most of Britain's cable tramways. These included the complex Edinburgh system on which they introduced many engineering innovations, mostly the work of W. N. Colam.

The Great Orme Tramway at Llandudno is worked by a cable in an underground conduit between the rails. The overhead trolley is for signalling purposes only.

This restored Douglas cable car is usually displayed at the depot, but on special occasions can be towed or propelled along the tracks of the promenade horse tramway.

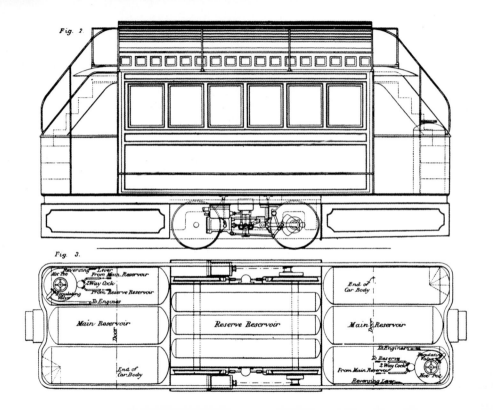

Fig. 2

Fig. 3.

Reversing Lever

Hot Pot

From Main Reservoir

2 Way Cock

From Reserve Reservoir

Regulating Valve

To Engines

End of Car Body

Main Reservoir

Door

Reserve Reservoir

Main Reservoir

Door

End of Car Body

To Engines

To Reserve

Regulating Valve

2 Way Cock

From Main Reservoir

Hot Pot

Reversing Lever

Mechanical Experiments

Of the various forms of motive power used on British tramways, only four (horse, steam, cable, and electricity from a power station) achieved a sufficiently widespread use to merit more than one picture in this book. Several other forms of motive power were tried at different times, some of which although not widely adopted in Britain were successful elsewhere. There were many short-lived experiments and demonstrations, but the examples chosen are those which were used in regular service.

Compressed-air tramways

The use of compressed-air as a form of motive power achieved its chief early success in the construction of railway tunnels through the Alps, where locomotives driven by compressed-air were used to haul the construction trains, their reservoirs being recharged from the mains that supplied the compressed-air rock-drills. On the locomotive, the air was fed through a reducing-valve to a set of cylinders and gear similar to that of a steam locomotive.

A Mekarski compressed-air tram tried in London in 1882. This drawing appeared in *Engineering*.

Compressed-air seemed to offer a very suitable form of motive power for tramways, being clean and quiet in operation. Patents were taken out in 1872 and 1873 by Louis Mekarski, concessionaire of the Nantes tramways in France, and Mekarski compressed-air cars or locomotives were later used in at least seven cities of France, including Nantes from 1879 to 1917 and Paris from 1887 to 1914. One of the Nantes cars is preserved in the Paris tramway museum. Steam-powered air-compressors were installed at the depots, from which the air was fed through underground mains to the terminus of each route, where the cars would stand and re-charge their reservoirs.

Two Mekarski locomotives were brought to Britain in 1880 and used for three months on the Wantage tramway, but were found uneconomic because the air-compressor used far more coal than would have been required to work the sparse service with steam traction. Another compressed-air car ran for a few weeks in 1881 between Stratford and Leytonstone, in London, and a Mekarski car was demonstrated in London in 1882. Five cars worked for four months in 1888 on London's Caledonian Road line, but in no case was operation on a sufficient scale to match the results achieved abroad. In similar trials at Chester, including some regular operation in 1890, it was found that more compressed-air was lost by leakage than used by the actual traction, so that the car could barely travel 3 km (2 miles) on the level on a single charge.

Tramway locomotives similar in principle to compressed-air cars were operated in Paris, Lille and Lyon on stored steam, and a tram was once built in New Orleans, USA, to run on compressed ammonia-gas, which being soluble in water could be absorbed after use in a water-tank for re-use later. A similar experiment was also carried out at Bolton in 1888, but in both cases the inevitable escape of ammonia caused the idea to be dropped.

Battery-electric tramcars

Many engineers experimented with tramcars fitted with electric accumulators, which appeared to offer the benefits of electric traction without requiring expensive fixed equipment. Trials began in Paris in 1881 and London in 1882, using converted horse cars, and a notable example was a bogie open-top accumulator car designed and built in London by Anthony Reckenzaun in 1884; this was the first tram to have two motors, series-parallel control, electrically-operated brakes, and trucks incorporating maximum-traction principles, features widely adopted later on electric trams.

Despite the many advantages, examples of regular service with accumulator trams in Britain are few. Battery locomotives hauled horse cars for some months in 1887–8 on London's Stratford–Manor Park line, and six double-deck cars were used from 1889 to 1892 between Greengate and Canning Town. The longest-lived operation was the Bournbrook line at Birmingham (1890 to 1901), and the last examples in Britain were two large bogie cars built for the Swansea and Mumbles line in 1903; these were later converted to trailers. British exports included eight battery cars for Australia; they too were not a success. Battery tramcars enjoyed a limited revival in the USA on short lines from about 1910 to 1920, and were used in more recent years on some rural tramways in Northern Italy.

In most early cases, the accumulators were mounted under the seats and changed through hinged panels in the side of the car, but fumes from the acid made the cars unpopular. Other drawbacks were the weight of the batteries, the need to re-charge them at frequent intervals, and the physical deterioration of the batteries. These factors combined to render battery traction more expensive than other forms, and led to its eclipse.

Mork
London
Loughborough
& Vienna

THE BRUSH ELECTRICAL ENGINEERING Co LD

Storage System

FALCON ENGINE AND CAR WORKS, LOUGHBOROUGH.

An accumulator tram built at Loughborough in 1889 for Australia, showing the hinged panels in the side of the car.

Gas-engined tramcars

Another form of mechanical traction tried on tramways was the gas-fuelled internal-combustion engine, operated either on mineral oil vaporized on the car, or on coal gas drawn from the town supply and compressed for storage in cylinders under the floor or seats. A battery or dynamo was fitted to provide spark ignition, and the cars had a large flywheel mounted in a circular casing beneath the floor or at one side of the body. The final drive was through a friction clutch and reduction-gearing.

The earliest experimental application was probably by F. Hurd of Edinburgh in 1880 using compressed town gas. The alternative oil-gas car originated in 1889 in the USA, where several 'Connelly gas motors' were used to haul horse cars. A similar oil-gas locomotive was tried in Croydon in 1893, and used in regular service on the London, Deptford & Greenwich Tramway from 1893 to 1895. Croydon also tried a Lührig car running on compressed coal gas, and similar cars were used at Dessau and Dresden in Germany. In 1896–7 the British Gas Traction Company introduced gas trams on the same principle at Lytham St Annes and Trafford Park; those at

A gas-engined tram in service at Lytham St Annes in 1897.

Lytham were replaced by electric cars in 1903, but operation at Trafford Park continued until 1908. Some Lytham gas cars were sold in 1899 to Neath Corporation, who operated them until 1920.

Uncompressed town gas has been used for internal-combustion road vehicles in times of wartime petrol shortage, and this method was used on the Heysham petrol trams in 1918.

Petrol-engined tramcars

Unlike most of the preceding examples, the tramcar powered by a petrol engine was a practical economic proposition, but few were used in Britain, since by the time reliable heavy-duty petrol engines had become available most of Britain's tramways had been electrified. The first vehicle was demonstrated by the Daimler company in Germany as early in 1888, and survives today in the Daimler-Benz museum at Stuttgart. Other early examples were built by the Fiat company of Turin, these and other cars being used mainly for internal transport at exhibitions.

Petrol-engined tramcars built by the Motor Rail Company of Bedford to the designs of John Dixon Abbott were supplied in quantity from 1910 onwards to the tramways of Karachi, and some of these cars, fitted with diesel engines, ran until 1975. At Stirling in Scotland a horse tram fitted with a petrol engine

A Leyland-engined petrol tram at Heysham in 1918, fitted for running on town gas owing to wartime petrol shortage.

ran from 1913 to 1920, and at Heysham four specially-built petrol trams with Leyland engines worked a sea-front service from 1912 to 1924. Petrol-engined trams have also been used on the Ryde and Ramsey pier tramways. Petrol or diesel-engined trams were introduced on many Continental

On the River Hospitals tramway near Dartford, internal transport between the isolation hospitals was by ambulance trams hauled by a motor vehicle.

The diesel-engined tourist tram that runs from Hans-sur-Lesse to the Grottes-de-Han in Belgium.

steam tramways, and some are still at work on the Grottes-de-Han tramway in Belgium. Some Netherlands tramways tried hauling former horse trams with petrol-engined road vehicles, and the same mode of operation was used until 1936 on the River Hospitals tramway at Dartford, with a Talbot motor ambulance pulling one or two ambulance trams.

The petrol-electric principle used for many years on motor-buses was also used briefly on four British tramways. The London County Council in 1912 fitted three horse cars with Tilling-Stevens petrol-electric propulsion for use on the Victoria Park—West India Docks route, but they never ran on the route for which they were designed, and were later adapted to shunt trailers at depots. Two petrol-electric winter cars were built in 1913–14 for Southend Pier, and petrol-electric tramcars were used at Hastings from 1914 to 1921 to replace the unsatisfactory surface-contact system along the Promenade (where overhead wires were not permitted). Two petrol-electric bogie cars were used in 1916–17 on the Dublin & Blessington Tramway, but were found to be underpowered. The same principle, but with a power unit of vastly greater output, is used in present-day main line diesel-electric locomotives.

Early Electric Trams

The great majority of tramways in Britain, as in other parts of the world, were eventually worked by electricity from a power station. Once their practicability had been established, electric tramways were installed in every large town of Britain, and many smaller ones, displacing the horse and steam trams, and facilitating the rapid extension of the tramways and the towns they served. This stage was, however, reached only after two decades of experiment.

The first electric tramway to provide a regular public service commenced at Berlin in 1881, but development proceeded much more rapidly in the United States than in Germany or elsewhere, and the early British installations which used methods derived from German practice were from about 1891 onwards rendered out-of-date by the availability of much more advanced equipment from America. From about 1896 onwards, almost all British tramcars had trucks and electrical equipment based on American designs.

British industry was quick to experiment with electric traction, and early inventors produced motors and mechanisms that often gave long years of service. Until the efficient overhead trolley method of current collection was introduced to

The electric pioneers (2) Side-mounted third rail on the Giant's Causeway tramway in Ireland, used from 1883 to 1899. The third rail is on the far side of the car.

The electric pioneers (1) Two-rail supply with positive and negative running rails on Volks Electric Railway at Brighton in 1886. The car was driven by a Siemens motor. In 1892 the supply system was changed to a third rail, as still used today.

VOLK'S ELECTRIC RAILWAY, BRIGHTON.

(The first public Electric Conveyance in the United Kingdom.)

How it is worked, and other interesting particulars.
PRICE ONE PENNY.

Britain in 1891, the current was supplied to the cars by other means. Volk's Electric Railway at Brighton (1883) initially used two-rail supply, Blackpool (1885) used underground conduit current collection, and third rail current collection was used at Giant's Causeway (1883), Bessbrook & Newry (1885), Carstairs House (1886), Ryde Pier (1886) and Southend Pier (1890) and on Volk's Railway from 1892. Overhead wires with rigid or semi-rigid bow collectors were used from 1893 in the Isle of Man, and from 1885 at a road crossing on the Bessbrook & Newry line. Two other methods tried on the Continent were a slotted overhead tube (1883) and a trolley carriage running on two wires (1882). But the trolley pole and wheel, when it arrived from America, proved so superior that it was used even for lines with British or German electrical equipment, such as Guernsey (1892) and the South Staffordshire Tramways (1893). The South Staffs Co. was also the first to use Alfred Dickinson's swivelling trolley head, which permitted a laterally displaced overhead wire; this became a characteristic feature of tramways in Britain and France.

The electric pioneers (3) The Holroyd-Smith underground conduit system at Blackpool, with a central slot.

The most serious fault with all early electric trams was that they were underpowered; the early motors proved unequal to the extra demand on starting from rest. At first only one motor was used on each car, but two became general after 1890. Transmissions were also at an experimental stage, and axle-mounted armatures, chain drives, worm drives and double-reduction spur gearing were all tried and later discarded in favour of single-reduction spur gearing, which became universal. The earlier 4-wheel cars had trunnion-type running-gear adapted from horse car practice, but in 1892 the Electric Construction Company produced the first British 4-wheel tramcar truck (for a Birmingham battery tram) and the Leeds Forge Company built some robust 4-wheel motor trucks with pressed steel side frames for the South Staffordshire Tramways, to the design of S. Fox. One of these trucks survives in the Science Museum reserve collection, and the design was widely copied in Germany and the USA. The separate truck, detachable from the car, quickly superseded the earlier method of fixing the motor to the car body.

The cars that housed these early experiments were copied either from the vehicles of the German electrical pioneers or from horse or steam tram practice, the latter predominating in the case of bogie cars. The South Staffordshire electric cars of 1892 were an exception to this, having plain arch roofs, transverse seats, and other features not generally adopted in Britain until a later period, though they resembled contemporary tramcars used in France, with the addition of a top deck. A Blackpool car of 1885 (retrucked in 1894 and re-equipped in 1899) is at the Tramway Museum, Crich, and an early Mather & Platt equipment is preserved in a Bessbrook & Newry car in the Belfast Transport Museum.

The device which did most for the electric tram was the spring-loaded trolley pole with a wheel running under a single overhead wire, invented by Charles Van Depoele in 1885 and perfected by Frank J. Sprague in 1887–8. It spread rapidly in America, giving its name there to the vehicle (the trolley) as well as to its current collector, and was introduced to Britain by the International Thomson-Houston Co., who in 1891 electrified a 3 km (2 mile) tramway at Roundhay, Leeds, and imported six American-built single-deck cars to work it. Other significant steps were Van Depoele's application of carbon brushes to traction motors in 1889–90, and the introduction in 1891 by the Westinghouse Co. of the first modern-type enclosed motor with four poles and four field coils instead of two.

The Thomson-Houston and Westinghouse companies soon secured contracts to electrify British

The electric pioneers (4) Alfred Dickinson's side-mounted trolley pole on the South Staffordshire Tramways, 1893.

A car and trailer of the period when most trucks and electrical equipment were imported from the USA. Car 8 and trailer 13 of the Douglas Southern tramway in the Isle of Man.

tramways, and the availability of reliable, standardized and proven American equipments ended the day when every installation was an experiment. Trucks, motors and control equipments were imported from America (the two principal suppliers of trucks were the Peckham Car Wheel Co. and the J. G. Brill Co.) and design improvements included nose-suspended motors, series-parallel control, and 'maximum-traction' bogie trucks, though both the latter features had already been used by Anthony Reckenzaun in his London battery-car of 1884. Properly-graduated speed control was now available, though braking was by hand except for an emergency electric brake which short-circuited the motors after re-connecting them as generators. Following the example set by Frank J. Sprague at Richmond, Virginia, American manufacturers had by this time standardized on 500 volts dc for traction equipment and this became the standard traction voltage in Britain.

Since Britain already had a well-established car-building industry, most of the American-equipped trams had British bodywork, though complete cars were imported from America for Bristol, Cheltenham, Devonport, Dublin, Liverpool and the Isle of Thanet tramways. Almost all cars were double-deck, but the steam tram practice of covering the top deck

was discontinued; the cover would have interfered with the trolley mountings, and anyway there were no more smuts. Owing to the light roof-construction, the trolley standard was usually mounted at one side of the top deck instead of at the centre.

Features perpetuated from horse cars included direct quarter-turn stairs, short canopies, internal monitors for ventilation, and oil lamps to protect the car in the event of a power failure. Tramways which relied mainly on pleasure-riding sometimes adopted the American type of open cross-bench car. Many undertakings experimented with trailers, and most used the Dickinson swivel-head trolley, though Glasgow, Douglas–Ramsey and a few others used the American-type fixed trolley head.

This 'American' period in electric trams is represented best by the Douglas Southern car at the Tramway Museum, Crich, which has Westinghouse (Pittsburgh) equipment and an American 'Lord Baltimore' truck of a type never manufactured in Britain. The museum also has two specimens of the Peckham 'Cantilever' 4-wheel truck, the type most frequently used at this period, and hopes to use one in restoring an 1899 tram from Hull.

A typical British electric car of 1898, mounted on an American-made Peckham cantilever truck. An oil headlamp was carried at night.

The British Electric Tram, 1901 to 1931

For about thirty years, roughly from 1901, the electric tram was the most widely used form of British urban transport, replacing the horse and taking the lead until overtaken by the trolleybus and motor bus after 1930. Thousands of electric cars were ordered and built between about 1901 and 1910 as the tramway systems were installed. After this the pace slackened, but additions to existing fleets brought the total number of tramcars in Great Britain to 14,481 in 1927, after which a decline set in. The cars built in this period were characterized by long life and high-quality timber bodies; they formed the majority of Britain's electric tramcars, and the majority of those preserved today in working or static museums. The traditions established in this thirty-year period remain as the most common 'image' of the traditional British tram.

The rush of orders after 1900 created good opportunities for manufacturers, and several new firms came into being. Foremost among these was the new Preston works of Dick, Kerr & Co., operated by

Four Dartford Council trams of the standard type built by the Dick, Kerr works at Preston. 3,000 of these cars were built for nearly 50 customers between 1900 and 1909.

two subsidiary companies, the Electric Railway & Tramway Carriage Works Ltd. who built the car bodies, and the English Electric Manufacturing Co. who supplied the electrical equipments. These companies were merged with others in 1905 to form the United Electric Car Co., which was absorbed in 1918 into the newly-formed English Electric Co. The Westinghouse Co. of Pittsburgh began in 1901 to make tramway motors and controllers at Trafford Park, Manchester, and the British Thomson-Houston Co. (British agents for the General Electric Co. of Schenectady, USA) set up its own works at Rugby. Wagon manufacturers Hurst, Nelson & Co. of Motherwell also made a successful entry into the tramway field at this time.

The success of American manufacturers in the British market did not go unnoticed on the Continent, and several Continental manufacturers also tried to gain a foothold in the British market. Two British firms (Witting Bros, Bruce Peebles & Co.) acted as agents for tramcar equipments produced by ACEC of Charleroi (Belgium) and by Ganz of Budapest respectively, but the only Continental manufacturer to remain active in Britain was Siemens Brothers, who had equipped the two pioneer lines of 1883. The British Westinghouse Co. became separated from its American parent company in 1917, and was re-formed as the Metropolitan-Vickers Electrical Co.; the British Thomson-Houston Co., however, remained under American control for another thirty years. In the 1920s another electrical group, the General Electric Co. of Great Britain, entered the traction field in partnership with the Oerlikon Co. of Zürich, Switzerland; no connection existed between this General Electric Co. and the similarly-named organization in America represented here in tramway days by British Thomson-Houston.

Of the tramcar builders active in horse and steam-tram days, the most adaptable proved to be the Falcon Engine & Car Works of Loughborough, which, after acquisition by the Brush Electrical Engineering Co. was associated with a large operating group (the British Electric Traction Co.) and developed into a large manufacturer of electric cars, second in output only to the Dick, Kerr group. G. F. Milnes & Co., whose old-established Birkenhead works could not cope with the demand, opened in 1900 a large new works at Hadley in Shropshire, but the enterprise failed in 1904. Another short-lived builder was the British Electric Car Co. of Trafford Park, active only from 1901 to 1904, which (with G. F. Milnes) was then absorbed into the United Electric Car Co. The younger branch of the Milnes family had meanwhile formed a specialist firm (G. C. Milnes,

Voss & Co.) to build tramcar fittings and top covers, and from 1905 also built complete cars, until closure occurred in 1913.

Although series-production techniques were necessary to cope with the demand, the cars which these firms built were characterized by high-quality craftsman-built timber bodies which if well maintained would last for at least twenty-five years. The renewal of worn parts was a straightforward job for an overhaul works, and cars could be given an extended lease of life by partial rebuilding to incorporate alterations in design; this practice became so widespread that the trams of the 'traditional' period (1901–31) which had remained in original state were later far outnumbered by those which had been altered, often more than once. This practice of 'upgrading' trams by reconstructing them was a mixed blessing, for while it saved money it also retarded progress in design. All too often, trams were rebuilt when they should have been replaced, and this led directly to the stagnation which seemed to set in after World War I, when the volume of new

A bogie car with reversed stairs built by the Brush Electrical Engineering Co. at Loughborough for the Wolverhampton District Tramways, a company in the British Electric Traction group.

Drilled plywood seats, petalled glass lampshades and patterned red glass half lights. A Manchester tram built in 1926.

Too many British trams were rebuilt when they should have been replaced. This one ran in Glasgow for 58 years (from 1899 to 1957) and covered 2,400,000 km (1,500,000 miles). It started life as an open-top car, and was twice rebuilt.

orders was insufficient to finance the research needed to produce new designs. The practice by some municipal undertakings of building cars in their own workshops further reduced the opportunities for the tramcar-building industry to continue its work of research and improvement. For too many British tramways, the traditional wooden car based on pre-1914 designs marked the limit of technical progress.

The type of car originally regarded as standard by all builders was the 4-wheel double-deck tram with open top deck and seating about forty-six to fifty persons; 8-wheel cars were less common. The plain arch lower saloon roof, introduced by the Preston works in July 1899 soon replaced the internal monitor roof except where a customer specified the contrary. The new form of roof was made possible by the increased strength of the car sides, corner pillars, and bulkheads. Ventilation was now by hinged 'half-lights' above the lower saloon windows, often of coloured glass, which gave a slightly ecclesiastical air to the interior of the lower saloon.

In the early deliveries the top deck extended only as far as, or slightly beyond, the lower saloon at each end, and the motorman therefore enjoyed no protection from the weather. On such cars the stairs generally rose directly through a quarter-turn from the platform to the top deck, as on horse cars,

though the London United Tramways (and a few others) adopted a stair with two short straight flights and an intermediate landing.

In June 1900, the Preston works in a batch of cars for Liverpool Corporation made a fundamental improvement by extending the upper deck to form two semi-circular canopies over the platforms. This feature, which permitted a greater seating capacity and afforded some weather-protection for the driver, was soon adopted by other builders, but required a new design of stairway if full use was to be made of the space thus gained. Two forms were used; many cars had a 'reversed' stair rising clockwise through 180° from the inner portion of the platform to the outer end of the canopy, but others had a 'direct' half-turn stair rising anti-clockwise through 180° from a point near the controller. The reversed stair was claimed as safer for the passengers, but even with perforated risers it obstructed the motorman's nearside view and for this and other reasons was not repeated in later designs; in London, its use was discontinued on the instructions of the police, and the cars thus equipped had to be

Motorman and conductor, Southend-on-Sea. Most pre-1914 British trams had open driving platforms.

altered. The half-turn direct stair remained standard for many years, but some towns returned to the quarter-turn stair of horse-tram days, which was easier to negotiate. A few operators also experimented with a straight stairway, mostly in later years.

Although most cars had open driving platforms, the extended canopy made it possible if desired to provide a windshield by fitting glazed panels between the canopy and the dash, and a few cars were built thus from 1901. Opinion was divided on the need for a windscreen, and although these became general in later years, many British trams ended their days without any such protection. In London this was due to police objections, but many operators (in the days before safety-glass) considered windscreens a source of danger in collisions. Tram-driving in those days was an outdoor occupation, and early photographs show drivers wrapped up in heavy greatcoats, with black oilskin capes when it rained. You could tell a senior driver by his face, bronzed and weather-beaten from the time he had spent on the open cars before the fitting of windscreens.

The next development was the provision of a top deck cover, which had temporarily disappeared with the demise of the steam tram. American electric

One of the first tramways to have enclosed driving platforms was the Tyneside company, in 1901.

tramway experience suggested that pleasure riding would be a major factor in revenue-earning, and the open top deck was the British equivalent of the American open car. Nevertheless, it is surprising that the covered-top electric car did not arrive sooner, for in wet weather, when riding tended to increase, the open top deck was thoroughly unpopular, and even the various types of 'dry-seat' (a turn-over seat usable after rain) represented only a limited improvement. Nevertheless, most British trams built before about 1906 began life with open top decks and spent some years in this form before acquiring top covers.

The first attempts to provide top deck passengers on electric cars with protection from rain and hot sun took the form of detachable canvas awnings, first tried (in Britain) at Liverpool in 1902. These were followed by roofs with sliding panels or roller blinds, and a few operators (mainly in Yorkshire) fitted top covers that could be lifted off again in the summer. Fixed top covers in several forms first appeared on British electric cars in 1903, but they did not become general in new construction, except in London, until some years later. Most tramways adopted a short upper saloon similar in length to the lower one and terminating short of the stairs and the end canopies. It was closed off at each end by a transverse bulkhead with a door.

The earliest form of short fixed top cover was devised by C. R. Bellamy, manager of the Liverpool Corporation Tramways, who by the end of 1904 had thus equipped most of the trams in his city. The 'Bellamy' top cover left the two ends of the top deck

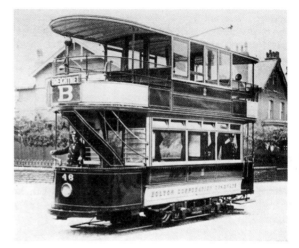

In 1903 the manager of the Bolton Corporation Tramways devised this 'open balcony' type of top cover. It was widely adopted during the next 25 years.

The alternative type of top deck cover, known as the 'Bellamy roof', on a tram built in 1915 for Wallasey.

SEACOMBE WARREN DRIVE. NEW BRIGHTON

WALLASEY CORPORATION TRAMWAYS

completely uncovered, but in most towns the roof was extended to form a canopy over each end of the top deck, converting these sections into roofed open balconies, typical of British tramways in late Edwardian days. Most of the British tramcars which received these open-balcony top covers retained them for the rest of their days, even after the design had become quite out-dated; where the cars were of narrow gauge (1067 mm or 1219 mm – 3 ft 6 in or 4 ft) and on single trucks, this was due to Board of Trade (later Ministry of Transport) regulations. Many operators also felt that the expense of a further alteration to enclose the end balconies was not justified by the small gain in covered capacity.

In London, the London County Council from 1906 onwards introduced a large fleet of bogie cars (classes E and E/1) with fully-enclosed top decks, and soon afterwards enclosed its earlier cars in similar fashion. By the end of 1910 the entire LCC double-deck tram fleet (under the stimulus of bus competition) had been provided with fully-enclosed top decks, and this example was gradually followed by tramways in the larger towns outside London during the next two decades, except for narrow-gauge and coastal tramways which tended to keep to the open top. A difficulty with the first enclosed-top cars was the draught which blew up the front

Top deck of a Croydon tram in 1942, showing the geared windows and the stairhead door. This wartime picture also shows blackout lampshades and anti-splinter window net.

stairway when the car was running. This was soon reduced by a hatch or trap-door, and LCC cars built from 1907 onwards were fitted with a full-height door and glazed draught-screen around the stairhead. The tradition of the partly-open top deck was often continued by fitting geared side windows that

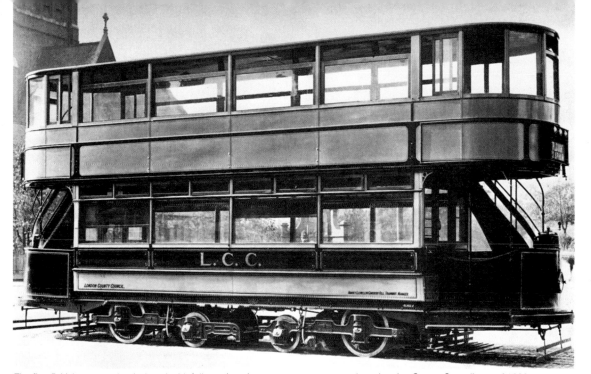

The first British trams to be designed with fully-enclosed top covers as new were these London County Council cars of 1906. 1,350 of these cars were built over the next 15 years.

could be lowered down to waist level in the summer if required.

Although double-deck trams predominated, some tramways had to use single-deck cars. The usual reason was restricted clearances, such as low railway bridges or London's Kingsway tram subway. In these cases it was usual to adopt long bogie cars so as to provide sufficient capacity to justify a two-man crew, and such cars frequently had either front-exit, or entrance/exit at both ends. Single-deck cars were also used on steep gradients, where the Board of Trade objected to the use of double-deckers with their higher centre of gravity, and on light railways such as the Grimsby & Immingham and the Blackpool & Fleetwood, where the adoption of single-deck cars enabled the line to qualify for the higher speed limit allowed on a light railway. Routes with light traffic were sometimes worked with one-man 'demi-cars' or by single-deck cars rebuilt from existing vehicles, and seaside or pleasure-resort tramways often used open cars with full-width cross-benches that gave a seating capacity little lower than that of a double-decker.

A single-deck tram built to negotiate low bridges on the Dearne District Light Railway, near Barnsley.

A 1904 one-man 'demi-car' at Gravesend. It ran until 1921.

Several design features were found only in single-deck cars. The cars often provided separate accommodation for smokers, either by an internal partition or by the use of combination cars, partly open and partly closed; in North America these were often known as 'California' cars, since they predominated in that State. The roof usually had a full-length glazed clerestory, which provided both ventilation and lighting, and another common feature was the narrow platform with single-width entrance. Most single deck cars had 'dwarf' trolley bases and unusually long trolley poles, but early cars often had trolley masts of the upright double-deck type, and the modern single-deck trams at Blackpool have trolley poles of normal length mounted on small steel towers.

The cross-bench cars form a class by themselves, and although in Britain they numbered fewer than 200 (as against the thousands used in America) they were firm favourites with visitors to the resorts they served. Narrow-gauge cross-bench cars usually seated four abreast, but standard-gauge examples such as the circular tour cars at Blackpool generally seated five abreast; these particular vehicles, shown on page 6, had the highest seating capacity of any British single-deck tram (sixty-nine). The use of cross-bench cars on street tracks gradually declined as increasing motor traffic added to the danger of step-board fare collection, but at Blackpool a central gangway was cut to ease the conductor's work. The Blackpool 'toastrack' cars were eventually replaced by modern open 'boat' cars with closed sides, but

'Combination' trams had a closed non-smoking saloon in the centre and open sections for smokers at each end. This one ran in Dundee. *Overleaf*

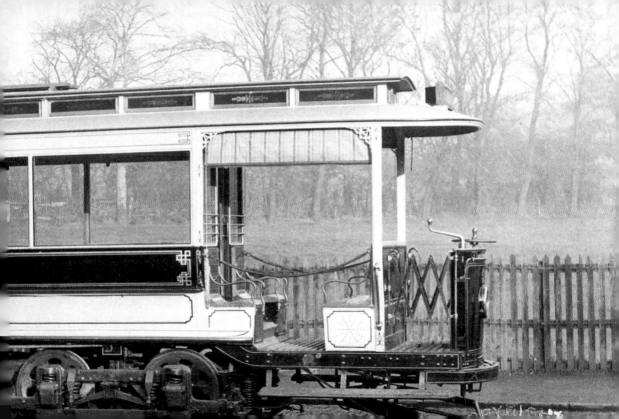

Wooden seats and a clerestory roof in a 1906 single-deck tram built to run through London's Kingsway tram subway. Double-deckers were used from 1931.

A cross-bench car and trailer of the Manx Electric Railway in 1979.

cross-bench cars still operate on the private-track Manx Electric Railway, with similar trailers, and form one of the Isle of Man's top holiday attractions.

Throughout the 1901–31 period, most British trams built for city service had wooden seats, both inside and out. Top deck passengers could usually face the direction of travel and observe the passing scene, but lower saloon passengers generally faced each other in two rows, usually on wooden slatted or perforated plywood seats without intermediate arm-rests. Transverse seats were the more popular with passengers, but operators were reluctant to use them on the lower deck, for the trams' restricted width and waisted side-profile would have required the use of two-and-one seating and would thus have reduced the total capacity. Several tramways tried using upholstered seating, but some discontinued it again on suspicion of harbouring vermin. The only widespread form of cushioned seating adopted on British tramcars before 1914 was that covered with cane rattan.

In London, the electric tramways faced competition from motor buses, which owing to their dependence on solid tyres had been using upholstered seats since they began. This competition finally forced the London tramways in 1925 to adopt transverse upholstered lower-deck seating; the

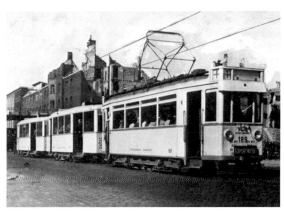

The use of trailer trams has always been normal practice on the European Continent. This three-car set ran in Hanover, Germany.

Upholstered transverse seating in a Glasgow bogie car of 1927. Thinner sides allowed a double seat on each side of the lower saloon gangway.

re-seated cars, described as 'Pullman trams' attracted many extra riders, and most London trams were thus equipped by 1931. Tramways outside London, most of which were less seriously affected by omnibus competition, were slow to follow this lead, and although a few operators followed the London example and adopted transverse seating, many others contented themselves with placing seat-cushions on the existing longitudinal seat-frames. Upholstered top deck seating (on covered cars) was even slower in coming, and relatively few examples existed until the late 1920s; the first large-scale user outside London was probably Edinburgh, from 1925.

The electric tramcar's reserve of power often enabled it to haul a trailer, and this has long been standard practice in Europe. About twenty British tramways adopted trailers at the time of electrification, using either converted horse cars or vehicles specially built, but most were soon withdrawn or converted to motor trams. The Board of Trade's regulations as to trailer brakes, requiring a separate brakesman, probably hastened their demise, except in Guernsey and the Isle of Man where these did not apply. In 1912, the London County Council obtained permission to reintroduce trailers, and 4-wheel open-top trailers were in use in South London from

1913 to 1924, when they were withdrawn to speed up the service. Trailer cars were supplied at the same period to Barrow, Greenock and York, but operation was equally short-lived. Modern light-weight trailers were introduced at Blackpool in 1960.

An interesting trend of the 1901–14 period was the building of special trams for non-passenger duties such as carrying stores or sand, removing snow from the tracks, spraying water to lay the dust, inspecting and renewing the overhead wires, or grinding out corrugations that formed on the surface of the rail. At this period, these 'works cars' were usually specially built for the purpose, and the larger manufacturers would offer standard types for each function. In later years the works cars were often old passenger cars demoted to departmental duties and more or less rebuilt in the process, a proceeding which often gave an extended lease of life to early types of car and finally permitted the restoration of some for museum purposes.

The concluding word in this section must be on destination indicators and liveries. Horse-trams normally remained on one route, and the names of the thoroughfares and districts traversed were painted on the vehicle. Steam, cable and electric trams at first followed the same practice, but as routes multiplied the route indications were shown on detachable and interchangeable boards, with separate boards or (in the case of electric trams) rotating stencil indicators to show the destination and direction of travel. From about 1902 these were mostly replaced by the illuminated linen destination blinds familiar today.

In an age when literacy could not be assumed, many passengers identified their horse car more by its colour and appearance than by the wording it bore, the cars often being painted in a different colour for each route. After 1900 this was less necessary, and electric trams generally bore a standard livery for each operator, but the practice survived at Glasgow and Aberdeen, where the upper deck panels of the cars were painted in distinctive colours to denote the route served. In Glasgow five colours were used (red, green, yellow, blue, white) and a Glasgow tram in the yellow route colour appears on the cover of this book. Another variation on this theme occurred in Plymouth, where a coloured disc was affixed to the dash panel to denote the route.

Supplementary route indicators in the form of coloured lights occurred on horse, steam, cable and

A sprinkler tram at work at Rochdale in 1912.

A London tram destination box of 1908. The three bullseyes denoted the route with coloured lights until the London County Council adopted service numbers in 1913.

electric tramways, Edinburgh being the most notable example. Several Continental cities, including Brussels and Amsterdam, still use differently coloured destination blinds for each route. Other British operators, such as Coventry and Exeter, employed route symbols. Route letters were sometimes used, two long-lasting examples being Hull and Bolton. Route numbers were introduced gradually from 1908 and were adopted by virtually all large

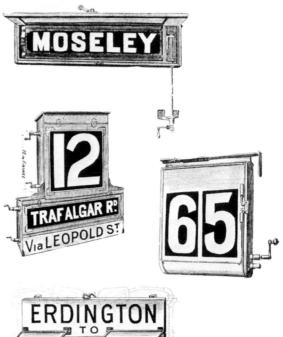

Destination and
Route Indicators

systems and many smaller ones. The route letters were at first painted on the cars or carried on plates. Later they, and route numbers, were usually shown by an illuminated stencil, until blinds were introduced for this purpose during the 1920s and 1930s.

Distinctive liveries for each tramway undertaking generally came in with electrification. A two-colour scheme was usual in Britain, the lighter colour being ivory, cream or primrose yellow, the other typically a brown or red, though various shades of blues and greens were favoured by many undertakings. Generally, the darker colour was applied to the dashes, waist panels, cant-rails, stair stringers and to the corresponding parts of the bulkhead. For contrast, the rocker panels, window frames and the side panels of the upper deck were normally painted in the light colour. Both colours were normally lined out round the edges; usually the darker colour was lined in gold leaf and the white or cream parts in a dark colour. In later years, when gold leaf became too expensive, it was simulated by tan, straw or yellow. A few tramways, such as Manchester, reversed the colouring of the waist and rocker panels.

Trucks, lifeguards and trolley masts were generally painted in a utility colour, such as red-oxide, and fenders and controllers were normally black. Those tramways which were still operating

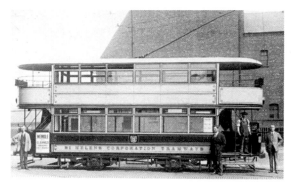

A traditional British tramcar livery (in this case, red and white) with the title along the rocker panel and the Corporation crest in the centre of the waist panel. This car also had a radial truck, in which the axles could pivot.

during World War II painted the fenders white, to be seen in the blackout, and several undertakings had to paint their trams grey or khaki. In Germany, the cross-country tramway at Herford painted its cars in camouflage, fawn dappled with brown and green. British trams were rarely disfigured by all-over advertising, though enamelled iron plates or paper bills were often fixed to the upper deck side and end panels. Several of those tramways which survived into the 1930s modernized their liveries by painting the rocker panels in the darker colour to match the waist panel, and Sheffield, Blackpool and Sunderland adopted attractive modern tram liveries.

In addition to the basic colours, a British tram had a wealth of detail in the form of lining, lettering, edging and coats of arms. The lining would often include a fancy panel repeated in each corner, and the waist panel might be divided into three or more separate panels, according to the number of side windows. Most trams in Britain carried the title of the undertaking in large gold letters on the light coloured rocker panel each side, with the lettering elaborately shaded in blue or red. It was a requirement that the name of the Manager or Secretary of the undertaking should appear on the side of the car, and this usually appeared in black letters in one corner of the rocker panel, below the gold title, with the manager's christian names in full.

By the latter part of the nineteenth century, most of the cities and municipal boroughs in Britain had adopted elaborate coats of arms and applied them to municipal buildings, stationery, street furniture, and municipally-owned vehicles such as tramcars. The coat of arms nearly always appeared in the centre of the waist panel, and was sometimes repeated elsewhere on the car, or etched in glass on the saloon door windows. A few tramways used a monogram instead of a coat of arms, and others used a garter device, sometimes surrounding a coat of arms or the car's fleet number. Companies in the British Electric Traction group displayed the group's 'Magnet and Wheel' device with the individual company's name around the magnet. In recent decades, heraldic transfers have become increasingly costly and their use on public service vehicles has declined.

A. L. C. Fell was manager of the London County Council Tramways from 1903 to 1924. His name appeared on about 1,850 trams and is remembered by such couplets as:

Aubrey Llewellyn Coventry Fell
When I ride on your trams I feel quite unwell.
They pitch and they sway and I get quite excited;
I'd much rather go on the London United.

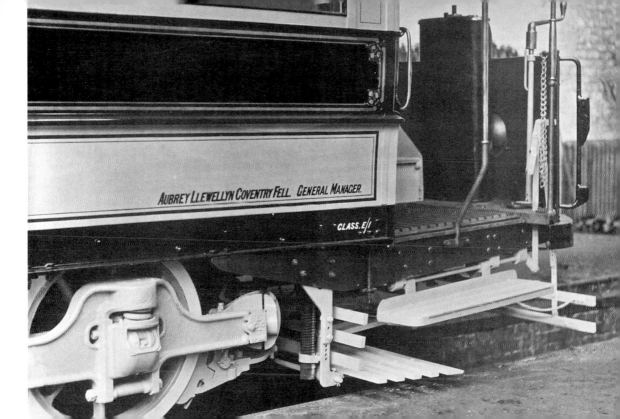

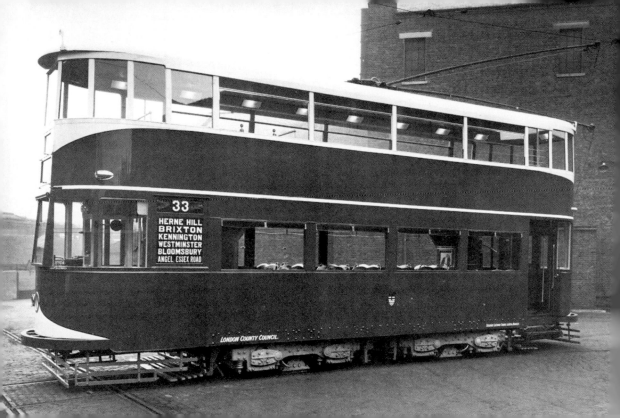

These two pictures show London's most modern tram, LCC No. 1, built at the Charlton overhaul works in 1932 and nicknamed Bluebird from its colour scheme. It later ran in Leeds, and is now preserved.

PART TWO
THE MODERN TRAM

Great Britain

The typical British tramcar of the mid-1920s was very similar to its pre-1914 predecessor. Very little had been done to bring the tramcar up to date, and practically no research was being done to improve it technically, apart from advances in motors and control equipment, derived partly from experience on urban railways. During this same period a rapid evolution took place in the design of buses and trolleybuses, and many tramways were in process of being replaced by these rubber-tyred vehicles.

Some cities, however, considered the tram to be the most suitable form of transport in their circumstances, and realized that the vehicles must compare in comfort and performance with the modern bus and trolleybus, which would mean discarding past traditions. The years 1930–3 marked a clear break between the traditional British tram and the modern British tram. Almost every feature of the car was re-designed, the new features generally including composite or all-metal bodywork, new types of truck, smaller wheels, lightweight motors of higher rating, roller-bearing axleboxes, air brakes, improved lighting, comfortable upholstered seats, and a smooth and generally rounded exterior without cornices and projections. Other innovations less generally adopted were rubber springing, platform doors, separate driving cabs, straight stairs, centre-entrances, glazed roof-lights, and air-operated contactor control.

The most fundamental programme of research into British tramcar design was that carried out by the Underground Group of companies in London in 1927–30 and resulting in the 'Feltham' type cars, which ran in North and West London until 1936–8 and then on the Streatham routes until they were sold to Leeds in 1951. One of them is now in the London Transport Museum at Covent Garden. In these trams, the possibilities of steel construction in permitting thinner sides and straight stairs, and dispensing with bulkheads, were the key to the design. The engineers of the London County Council and the English Electric Company were engaged in similar research programmes, culminating in LCC car No. 1 of 1932 and Blackpool No. 200 of 1933. Important experiments in all-metal bodywork were also carried out at Edinburgh, and almost all subsequent British tramcars embodied features from one or more of

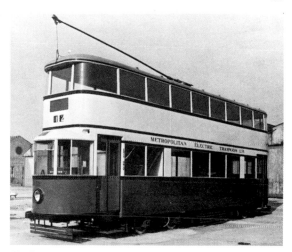

The first prototype 'Feltham' tram, No. 320 of Metropolitan Electric Tramways Ltd. at the Union Construction Company's works at Feltham, Middlesex. 100 similar trams ran in London until 1950–1 and were then sold to Leeds.

these experimental cars. Unfortunately, there was no such thing as a standard modern British tram; each town developed its own idea of what the modern tram should be, and insisted on its own design

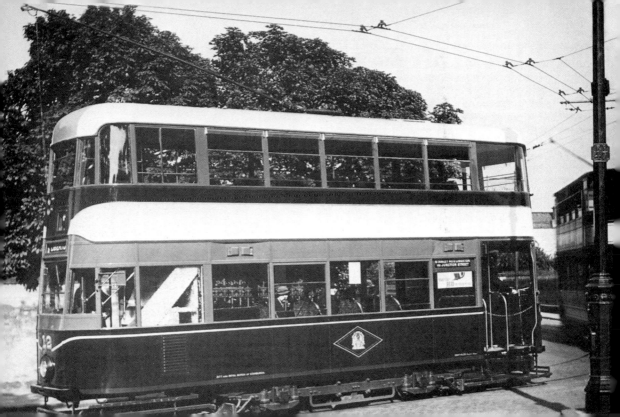

even when a manufacturer offered a lower price for another type already in production, such was the strength of civic pride.

Since all-metal or mainly-metal body construction required more specialized plant and processes than did timber construction, the trend towards constructing cars in overhaul workshops was now reversed, and many of Britain's modern trams were built by the specialist manufacturers. Fortunately the two leading firms (English Electric and the Brush Electrical Engineering Co.) had both entered the bus body field, and had thus maintained their body-building works. The London 'Feltham' trams were built by the Union Construction Company, a subsidiary of the Underground Group set up for the purpose and specializing in all-steel vehicles, a form of construction which was compulsory for the tube railways.

After 1945 these firms no longer built trams, and operators requiring new trams were supplied by railway rolling-stock manufacturers such as R. Y. Pickering & Co., Charles Roberts & Co., and Metropolitan-Cammell; two prototype trams for Leeds were built by a bus body builder, C. H. Roe of Leeds. Four operators did however re-tool their workshops to produce composite-bodied tramcars – the Corporations of Liverpool, Sheffield, Edinburgh and Glasgow – and these continued to turn out new trams until 1940, 1946, 1951 and 1955 respectively.

All-metal construction had been adopted on a fairly wide scale in the USA by about 1925, and allowed a more spacious and flexible interior layout. The first British tram to derive any advantage from this was an experimental Glasgow single-deck car of 1926, now in the Glasgow Museum of Transport. After 1930, the rising cost of high-grade timber caused a general change to part-metal construction, a common method being composite bodywork with teak framing and steel or aluminium panels, the latter adopted from bus practice. The use of smooth, rounded exterior forms, gave a result akin to streamlining, though this could have no practical effect at the speeds allowed.

The use of a strong body shell removed the need for interior bulkheads, and enabled the stairways to be wider, straighter and less steep. The front stairway could if necessary be separated from the driving position, to permit its use by the conductor and (in front-exit cars) by passengers wishing to alight. American experience also focused attention on the

Another early user of all-metal bodywork was Edinburgh. These cars were built in 1934.

possibilities of the central entrance, which could be brought lower and thus nearer to ground level, and enabled the conductor to spend more time on the platform; this was adopted on several classes of modern British trams, sometimes with air-operated sliding doors under the control of the driver. In some Continental countries all-metal bodywork for tram-cars has been made compulsory, to give the passengers greater protection in collisions with other road vehicles.

A tram was usually quite well lit, for there was plenty of electricity available, but the value of good lighting in attracting riders was only fully exploited after about 1925, the London County Council tram-ways again taking the lead. The practice of using white ceilings also dated from this period. Good lighting was a feature of all modern British trams, and several types also incorporated curved glass roof-lights, first introduced on trams at Blackpool in 1933 and taken from luxury motor-coach practice. In 1946–7 fluorescent lighting was tried in three British trams, but this did not become general at that time.

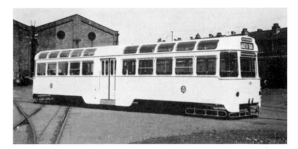

Three types of streamlined tram built by English Electric, Preston for Blackpool Corporation in 1934. They were built to last; some are still running today.

Curved glass 'roof-lights' were a popular feature of many British trams built after 1933. The photographs above show a Blackpool trailer built by Metropolitan-Cammell in 1960.

Aberdeen Corporation, like Blackpool, preferred the centre-entrance. Twenty-two of these modern bogie trams ran there until 1958.

remaining horizontal; later examples used foam-rubber cushions as in bus practice. The cars usually had chromium-plated or stainless-steel fittings in place of brass, plastic interior panelling in place of wood, and linoleum or rubber floor-coverings in place of slats. A seat was provided for the driver wherever police regulations allowed, and even where he was not given a separate cab, folding or sliding platform doors were usually provided to enclose the forward platform. Cars built after 1946 generally employed rubber-mounted windows which could be replaced easily, another feature taken from bus practice. Finally, almost all modern British trams were given a simpler and brighter livery than their predecessors.

Another feature of the modern British tram was the first really comfortable type of upholstered swing-over seat, introduced by G. D. Peters & Co., with the seat cushion tipping backward instead of

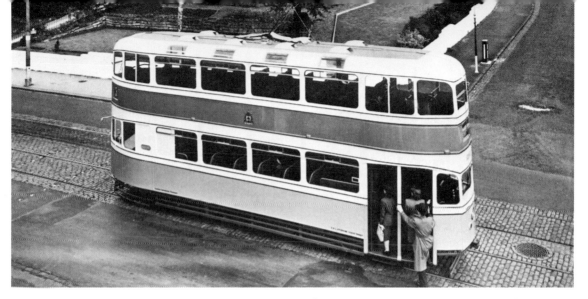

One of the principal British users of modern trams was Glasgow Corporation. They were built in the Corporation's own workshop at Coplawhill, and were claimed as 'the finest short-stage vehicles in Europe.' The first 152, known as the 'Coronation' type, entered service between 1937 and 1941, and a further 100 'Mark Two' cars of the type shown in this photograph were built in 1948–52. The colour scheme was green, cream and orange. They were renowned for their speed and smooth riding, and because a railed vehicle can carry a substantial overload, they had a well-remembered notice that 'There shall be no limit on the number of standing passengers carried on the last car on any route.' Most of the modern Glasgow trams remained in use until 1962, often with women drivers.

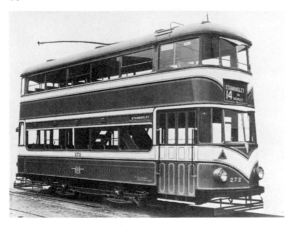

Liverpool Corporation built 263 streamlined double-deck trams at its Edge Lane works between 1936 and 1942, and ran them until 1957. They included the fastest trams in Britain, which when running on the reserved grass tracks laid down the centre of suburban avenues frequently overtook private cars in the adjacent carriageway. The high speeds were due partly to their lightweight construction, and most of them had to be expensively reconditioned after about twelve years service. When new, they were nicknamed 'Green Goddess' cars after a popular melodrama, olive green being the main colour of their livery. They were replaced by buses in 1954–7 and their former express tracks are now ornamental grass strips with shrubs down the centre of suburban Liverpool's dual-carriageway roads. *Right*

Leeds City Transport had some very distinctive modern trams, of several types. The finest were seventeen bogie cars built for the express tramway to Middleton, which had its own private track away from the roads, climbing up through Middleton Woods. There were three similar 4-wheel cars, the first of which (No. 272) is shown here when new in 1934. Development continued until 1953, but rising costs then caused the city council to switch to buses, and the last trams ran in 1959.

The most luxurious trams built for use in Britain were the twenty 'Railcoaches' for Blackpool built in 1937 by the Brush Electrical Engineering Company at Loughborough. They had deep-cushioned moquette seats, opening sunshine roofs, ornamental Alhambrinal ceiling panels, eight-day clocks, patterned rubber floors, curved glass roof-lights, and alternate window-posts were trimmed in polished stainless steel. They ran in this form for an average of 2 million km (1¼ million miles) and were then mostly withdrawn or rebuilt, but one has been put aside as a memento, and is awaiting restoration.

Sunderland, where it joined seven similar cars. Because of high winds experienced on the coast road between Roker and Seaburn, Sunderland trams collected their current by a railway-type pantograph, shown in this photograph. Some of Sunderland's tram pantographs are used today on the National Coal Board's electric trains in South Shields, but the trams themselves were scrapped in 1953–4.

Sunderland and South Shields had some 4-wheeled modern trams, shorter versions of the big centre-entrance cars used in Blackpool and Aberdeen. This one was built by the Brush company for South Shields in 1936, but when South Shields changed over to trolleybuses ten years later they sold it to

The last new 4-wheel trams built for a British city were for Sheffield. This one, No. 501, was built by the Corporation in 1946, followed in 1950–2 by thirty-five similar cars by railway wagon builder Charles Roberts & Co. of Horbury near Wakefield (they were known as the 'Roberts' cars). 501 was the first British tram to have fluorescent lighting. The cream livery with blue bands was chosen by the city council in the 1930s to brighten up the image of their city with its concentration of heavy industry. Sheffield's trams were good examples of modern vehicle architecture, neat and functional yet with no exaggerated streamlining. Above the car is the triangle of wires known as an automatic trolley reverser, defined in the glossary.

Trams, being self-steering, can run safely in tunnels, including subways built under city streets. Several Continental cities have built tram subways as an alternative to underground railways; in the suburbs, the trams emerge to run on sleeper tracks alongside the roads. In 1944–5 the city of Leeds drew up plans for two cross-city tram tunnels under the central shopping area, and later arranged for C. H. Roe & Co. to build two prototype subway trams, 601 and 602, to test new kinds of equipment. They were built in 1953 and painted in royal purple and cream. Unfortunately, there was never enough money to build the tram tunnels, and the people of Leeds now ride in standard diesel buses. 602, possibly the quietest tram ever tried in Britain, now runs at the Tramway Museum in Derbyshire.

Not all post-war trams have been modern or stream-lined. Those built to work on the new tourist tramway between Seaton and Colyton in Devon are mostly half-size replicas of Edwardian open-top trams that ran in Bournemouth, Llandudno or North London. This one, No. 8, was built in 1968 and can seat 41 passengers. The 838 mm (2 ft 9 in) gauge track is laid alongside the estuary of the River Axe and the ride is especially popular with bird-watchers; fifty-three varieties of British birds have been observed in a single day from the cars of the Seaton and District Tramway, and naturalists and bird-watchers sometimes hire special cars on Saturday and Sunday mornings, stopping for a while along the line while the passengers identify and log the different species. The trams run so quietly that the birds have become quite used to them, and take little notice.

Another recent 'replica' tram is No. 5 of the Snaefell Mountain Railway in the Isle of Man. It was built in 1971 by boatbuilder Kinnin of Ramsey to replace a vehicle lost by fire, and was deliberately built to resemble the original Snaefell cars of 1895. All six Snaefell trams now have bogies built by London Transport's railway works in 1977–8, and modern German electrical equipment that allows them to descend the 620 m (2,036 ft) mountain using friction-less electric (rheostatic) braking. Because of the high winds on the mountain-top they still have special rigid 1895-type current collectors.

The 18-km (11-mile) coast tramway from Blackpool to Fleetwood is now worked mainly by these one-man trams built in the Corporation's workshops in 1972–6 and incorporating the frames, bogies and electrical equipment from older vehicles built by English Electric, Preston, in 1934–5. To make room for the ticket machine on the driver's left, the controller in these cars is worked by the driver's right hand, the reverse of the usual arrangement. In summer, several other types of tram supplement the one-man cars and the Corporation takes on students as seasonal conductors.

Blackpool's newest tram at the time of writing is double-decker 761, built in the Corporation's own workshop in 1979. It seats ninety-eight passengers (fifty-four upstairs, forty-four downstairs) and has end sections of a type mass-produced for motor buses. Trams of this size would have been too large for most British cities, but the promenade line at Blackpool runs in a straight line for 11 km (7 miles); the only sharp curves are at terminal points. 761 has Westinghouse thyristor control gear, a new form of equipment which controls the current to the motors on the 'chopper' principle instead of by the traditional resistors. This equipment gives a useful saving in current consumption.

The Tram Abroad

So far, much of this book has been in the past tense, because trams and tramways are now a rarity in Britain, where most city transport is provided by double-deck diesel buses which the rest of the world finds rather quaint, and rarely copies. On the Continent, and in some other countries, trams in their modern form are still the favourite form of city transport on really busy routes. In this book, space does not permit mention of more than a small sample of the many different types in use around the world, but the selection that follows will suffice to show that the tram is alive and well. Unfortunately, none of them are now made in Britain (the last tramcar exports were to Khartoum, in 1952) because the British industry, lacking a home market, turned to other products.

Building trams for export, particularly to South America, was for many years an important British industry. This 1912 open car was one of fifty built by Hurst Nelson & Co. of Motherwell for the city of Santos tramways in Brazil; the makers were still supplying spare parts for them forty years later. More than half of all the trams exported from Britain went to South America; other countries supplied from Britain were Egypt, Greece, South Africa, New Zealand, India, Burma, Malaya, China and Japan. Tramcar trucks and electrical equipment were also shipped out to Australia, Canada, Norway, France, Holland, Finland, Spain and Portugal for trams with locally-built bodies.

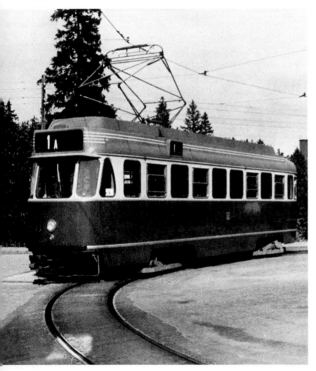

Motors and control gear for trams were still being made in Britain in the 1950s, when the A.E.I. works in Trafford Park, Manchester, supplied the electrical equipment for these modern green trams now running in the Finnish capital, Helsinki. Like most modern trams, they are single-ended, with doors on one side only, and therefore need turning circles at each end of the route. The newest trams in Helsinki are two-section articulated cars built entirely in Finland. *Left*

The most advanced trams of the 1940s were these 'PCC' cars in North America. The initials stand for 'Presidents' Conference Committee', the industry association that decided to sponsor a research programme into tramcar design and produce a vehicle for the future. Many thousands were built, and some still run in Boston, Philadelphia, Pittsburgh, Cleveland, Newark, Toronto and San Francisco. Special features included rubber-sandwich resilient wheels for silent running, noiseless gears, and a new control system that gave completely smooth acceleration and braking. The design principles were copied by the Belgian tramcar industry after the war and similar cars with European bodies now run in Belgium, Holland, France and Yugoslavia. *Right*

In Europe, the first country to introduce a standard modern tram was Switzerland. The Association of Swiss Transport Undertakings drew up standard designs in 1941–2 and sufficient new cars were built in the next two decades to replace almost all the older trams running in Basle, Berne, Zürich and Geneva. Some were lightweight vehicles for solo running, others were heavier and designed to pull trailers. They are single-ended and were originally arranged for rear-entrance/front-exit, with the conductor seated at a cash desk. Today, the Swiss tramways all use self-service roadside ticket machines, and the trams are worked by one man. The oldest of these standard cars are now being replaced by new articulated cars, but most will be running for several years yet. A notable feature was Brown Boveri 'Simplex' trucks with springborne motors and cardan-shaft drive.

For many years, the most 'tram-minded' country of Europe was Belgium, where the tram was used not only for city transport but also for cross-country routes, run by a single nationwide undertaking (SNCV/NMVB) known colloquially as the 'Vicinal'. The newer cars were built in their own workshops, and often pulled one, two or more trailers. The modern decline in rural transport demand caused many lines to close, but there is still an extensive network around Charleroi and La Louvière, of which one line passes through this tunnel at Mariemont. The best-known line to British holidaymakers is the 64 km (40 mile) express tramway along the Belgian coast which connects at Ostend with the ships to and from Dover, and will be re-equipped with new cars in 1980–1.

France has only a few tramways, but is planning to reintroduce them in two cities – Nantes and Strasbourg – and may do so elsewhere. Meanwhile, Lille has two fast interurban tram routes to Roubaix and Tourcoing, Marseille has a tram subway route worked by Belgian-built PCC cars (see page 103) and similar trams, shown here, run in St Etienne. St Etienne uses them because it has an unusually narrow main street, sufficient for just three lines of traffic, in which the trams with their narrow gauge tracks and automatic steering can run safely close-in to the kerb and so make the maximum use of the road space. Modern trams very similar to those shown also run in the Belgian cities of Brussels, Ghent and Antwerp, and the Dutch city of Den Haag (The Hague).

The electric tram was a German invention. The first demonstration line ran in a Berlin exhibition in 1879 (hence the Centenary of Electric Traction events in 1979) and the first public service began in a Berlin suburb in 1881. German law gave trams priority over other road users and allowed them to run in trains, usually of three cars in large cities and two cars elsewhere. Almost all the trams were 4-wheelers until the 1950s, but the newest ones included some quite modern designs, like Bochum 550 of 1942 here contrasted with one of the same company's first electric trams of 1899. A simplified utility version of this design was built from 1944 to 1948 to replace the many trams lost in wartime bombing.

spectacular increases in tram-riding, sometimes up to 40 per cent. Ticketing is self-service; multi-ride cards or ticket books are on sale at shops and kiosks, and one ticket per ride must be inserted in a canceller on the vehicle, which stamps the route, date and time and rings a bell. No conductors are carried, but there are roving inspectors who can fine you on the spot if your ticket is not validated.

Most West German trams built since the mid-1960s have been articulated vehicles, with two or three jointed sections which follow the curves in the track. Each one can carry from 200 to 250 passengers, replacing the older trains of a motor tram with two trailers. In some cities they now run underground in the city centre, avoiding the traffic jams, and cities which have built these tram subways have reported

The world's most prolific tram-building country is Czechoslovakia, where the CKD-Tatra factory in Prague turns out thousands of these 'Tatra' trams for the cities of Eastern Europe and the Soviet Union. The examples shown here, of two different types, are in Kiev, USSR. The first modern Tatra trams were tried in Prague in 1951, and they gradually replaced every other type used in their home country. In Kosice, Slovakia, they operate Europe's fastest tramway, an express cross-country line linking the town with the East Slovakian Steelworks near the Russian border. Tatra trams are also a common sight in East Germany, but there they are usually painted cream instead of red. Their electrical control system is similar to that of the American-designed PCC car.

The world's largest tram systems are those of Vienna, Leningrad, and Budapest. Vienna's trams resemble the modern German types and are built under German licence, but Budapest has some distinctive designs created by the Ganz electric works in conjunction with the Budapest city transport undertaking. The 8-wheeled type on the left was built in the 1940s and 1950s, the right-hand one is a newer articulated car. For many years Budapest had the most intensive tram service in the world – the No. 6 route, with a train of three cars running every fifty seconds at peak hours. Budapest today has an underground railway to carry the heaviest traffic, but the trams are still busy, and similar heavy traffic is carried on trams in Warsaw, Poland.

Apart from Blackpool, only one place in the world now uses double-deck trams, namely Hong Kong. They were built in local shipyards about thirty years ago, replacing older double-deckers, and are well suited to the hot, humid climate because riding upstairs with the drop-windows open gives a welcome breeze. Until 1972 the top deck was first class, at a higher fare, but today you pay the same (bargain) fare upstairs or down. There are also some single-deck trailers. Double-deckers were also used until quite recently in Alexandria, Egypt, but have been replaced by new single-deckers built in Japan.

Japan's trams are not as modern as its electric trains, but there are quite a lot of them in the medium-sized cities (the really big cities have replaced them with underground railways). This two-section articulated car, painted salmon-pink with a red waistband, runs in Hiroshima and provides a through service from the city on to a suburban electric railway. In Japanese trams the driver announces the stops through a microphone clipped to his cap, and sometimes uses a cassette recorder to play advertising jingles. There is usually a flat fare with a coin-box, but in one city (Kitakyushu) you take a boarding-ticket from a machine and then pay the appropriate fare to the driver as you get off, according to how far you have travelled. *Left*

In Melbourne, Australia, the newest trams are known as Z-cars and are painted a bright orange, contrasting with the dark green of the older types. Melbourne has many miles of tramway, some quite new, and although the tracks are laid in the street, the passengers board the cars from safety-zones like the one in the foreground. Traffic in Australia keeps left, as in Britain and Japan. Each tram still carries both a driver and a conductor, with variable fare stages as in Britain. The other Australian city using trams is Adelaide. *Right*

The latest development in European city transport is the 'Stadtbahn', midway between tramway and underground railway. These green trains in Hanover can run in the street, on reserved sleeper tracks, or in the underground sections beneath the city centre, which have railway signals and full-size stations. The cars have folding steps, and can use either high or low platforms. The tramways in the Ruhr cities are gradually being upgraded into a regional network of Stadtbahn lines, with another network around Cologne and Bonn. Stadtbahn systems provide the benefits of an underground railway network at considerably lower cost, and served as the model for the Tyne & Wear Metro at Newcastle.

PART THREE
TECHNICAL
References are to electric trams unless otherwise stated.

Car Building

Underframe

The basis of a tram is the main underframe, which serves as a moving platform on which to build the body. The principal parts are the solebars (the longitudinal members along the sides) and the headstocks (the transverse members across the ends) which together form a stout rectangular frame on which the floor and the walls of the car are then built. The wheels, motors and brake gear are made separately and fitted later. The underframe has additional cross-members in the middle, and the end platforms of a traditional tram are built on 'platform bearers' cantilevered out from the main frame and ending in a steel fender that allows one tram to push another. In modern trams, the use of small wheels and motors allows a lower floor level and eliminates the need for cantilevered platforms. Horse trams and early electric trams had teak underframes, but steel soon became usual.

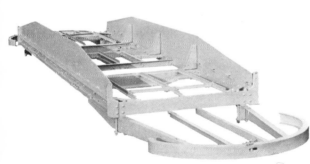

Underframe built by Hurst Nelson & Co. for a metal-bodied London tram of 1929 (LCC 1853).

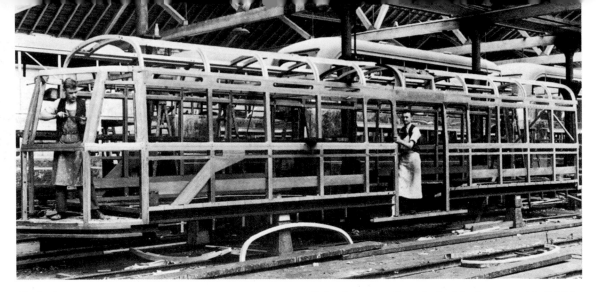

Body frame

Teak-framed bodies were usual until the 1930s (this one was built in 1937 for Blackpool Corporation by the Brush company at Loughborough), though by that time mahogany side panels had been replaced by steel or aluminium. Steel-framed bodies began to be built from 1930 onwards, but did not become general in Europe until after 1945. Oak, ash, teak and pitch-pine were the principal timbers used in British trams, though lighter woods had been used in horse cars. The upright members are window pillars and corner-pillars, the main longitudinal members are the waist rail (divided in this case by the centre-entrance) and the cant rail above the windows. The car ends are curved or tapered to provide clearance between cars on curves.

Trucks

Single trucks

A peculiarity of electric trams was that their trucks, which contained the wheels and motors, were generally supplied by a different firm from that which made the body. The type in most widespread use in Britain for 4-wheel trams was the 21E 4-wheel truck patented by the J. G. Brill Company of Philadelphia, USA. The superiority of the 21E truck was such that other firms who had produced their own types of 4-wheel truck (Hurst Nelson & Co., Mountain and Gibson, and the Brush company) were eventually obliged to build the Brill type instead, with minor differences. These trucks had a solid forged frame and were produced with a wheelbase of 1·8–2·3 m (6 ft to 7 ft 6 in), according to the length of the car body to be supported. After the first few years, a trend towards longer 4-wheel cars created a need for a longer truck wheelbase, to give adequate support to the body, but the track curves would not permit this unless the axles were free to pivot in relation to the truck or car frame. A search began for a satisfactory radial-axle design, and many different patented designs were tried from about 1904 onward, such as the Conaty & Lycett, the Mountain & Gibson, Warner's Patent, and the Brill Radiax.

None achieved lasting success, for their radiating properties deteriorated quickly with wear, and their steel tyres would wear out about four times more quickly than those used in conventional trucks. An alternative solution was found after 1912 in the Peckham pendulum type of truck which allowed the axles to move laterally independently of the truck frame. 4-wheel British trams built after 1930 generally used the Electro-Mechanical Brake Company's 'hornless' truck, in which the axle was carried by strong leaf-springs that would both flex and twist, or the Maley and Taunton truck with swing-link axle suspension.

Maximum-traction bogies

For longer trams, it was necessary to use two bogie trucks. In Britain, these were usually of the single-motor maximum-traction type, with one motored and one pony axle, the motored axle having larger wheels than the other and carrying most of the weight. This type of truck combined bogie riding qualities with the simplicity and low cost of two-motor equipment. The design most widely used at the outset was the Brill 22E bogie, but other types produced by G. F. Milnes, McGuire, Brush, Peckham and Hurst Nelson were also used. Some were 'reversed', with the small wheels towards the ends of the car (as in these Hurst Nelson examples) but most had the small wheels towards the car centre. The size of the electric motors meant that the trucks had to be mounted under the body rather than under the platforms. The loading of the pony wheels was often increased on curves by a spring pillar moving in an inclined track.

Swing-bolster trucks

From 1906 onward, most tramway undertakings using bogie cars adopted one or other of two British truck designs evolved specifically for heavy double-deckers, the London County Council Class 4 bogie truck of 1906 and the Burnley truck of 1909. The LCC Class 4 truck shown in the upper picture was evolved by the engineers of the London County Council Tramways from a truck designed by the McGuire company of Chicago and manufactured in Britain by Mountain & Gibson Ltd. of Bury. Its most important feature was a swing bolster, a railway practice which permits some lateral play between the car body and the truck. The space between the axles was occupied by the bolster and the motor was therefore placed in the outside-hung position, where it would also give better adhesion properties. An attempt by the LCC Tramways to extend the use of this feature to 4-wheel cars (as in the lower photograph) was unsuccessful; the 100 cars concerned had to be fitted with side swing dampers after a few years. Plough carriers for underground conduit current collection were fixed to each type of truck, as shown.

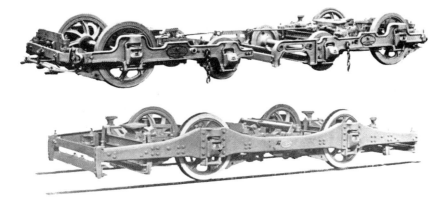

The Burnley truck

The Burnley truck was devised by the manager of the Burnley tramways, H. Mozley, who added pony wheels to a Simpson & Park radial truck, and by re-positioning the side bearing springs enabled up to 80 per cent of the weight of the car to be carried on the driving wheels. The largest single user of these trucks was the Birmingham Corporation.

Tramcars with maximum-traction bogie trucks were more common in Britain than in any other part of the world. About 4,000 were built, including most of those which ran in London, Birmingham and Man-chester. The maximum-traction type of truck was particularly well suited to double-deck cars, since a pivotal point displaced towards the driving axle reduces the lateral displacement of the large driving wheels and allows the side-sills of the car to be carried low, with a consequent reduction in the height of the car. On the Continent, where single-deck trams with a high floor level were traditional, pivotal trucks for 4-wheel cars were made to work successfully and little use was made of maximum-traction bogies; good results have also been obtained with 6-wheel trucks, which apart from two isolated experiments were never used in Britain.

Equal-wheel bogie trucks

In North America, the typical tramcar of the pre-1930 period was a long bogie vehicle with four motors, mounted in two equal-wheel trucks adapted from railroad practice. Some British operators used similar equipments, but in certain cases the four motors were replaced by two motors of higher output, leaving the other two axles not driven. Experiments to couple them with chains or coupling-rods were unsuccessful, as were the English Electric company's attempts in 1929–31 to produce a monomotor bogie with double-ended drive. A few operators in towns without hills, such as Blackpool, used two-motor equal-wheel trucks from the start, despite the slightly lower adhesion obtained; the bolster centres could either be located centrally between the axles or slightly nearer the driving axle. The picture shows one of the English Electric equal-wheel single-motor trucks supplied to Blackpool in 1934, which are still in use today, some modified with chevron-type rubber springs. Other British equal-wheel tramcar trucks of the 1930s were made by Maley & Taunton Ltd. and the Electro-Mechanical Brake Co.

Modern trucks

The final developments in the single truck were the adoption of resilient gears and rubber springing, and the use of smaller motors and wheels to allow a lower floor level. Much greater technical advances were made in the design of bogie trucks, and these marked a new period of American influence in European tramcar design. The revolutionary Presidents' Conference Committee (PCC) car of 1936 had high-speed motors mounted at right angles to the axles, a high gear ratio with silent spiral-bevel gears, and resilient rubber-insert wheels. The bogies had inside frames to allow the individual replacement of resilient wheels, and friction braking was on separate braking drums or discs. These features and the automatic multi-notch control gave a performance claimed to be superior in acceleration, smoothness and quietness to any other form of transport.

A licence to manufacture this equipment in Britain was obtained in 1945 by Crompton Parkinson Ltd., while Maley & Taunton Ltd. produced an inside-frame PCC-type truck. In Britain, Blackpool was the only tramway to make widespread use of these improvements in tramcar design, but they have been widely adopted on the Continent. The picture shows a resilient-wheel PCC-type truck under a Brussels

tram, with a battery-operated magnetic track-brake shoe between the wheels. The most recent European type is the Düwag monomotor truck, in which a single centrally-mounted longitudinal motor drives both axles.

Wheels

Until about 1902, most British trams followed American practice in using chilled cast-iron wheels, which were of low first cost but would last for only about 48,000 km (30,000 miles). Experiments took place on the South Staffordshire tramways in 1894 with steel tyres shrunk on to separate wheel-centres; these tyres could be turned on a lathe to restore the correct profile and replaced by new tyres when worn down, as in locomotive practice. Steel-tyred wheels came into general use on British tramways after about 1903, the previous standard size of 762 mm (30 in) being increased to 813 mm (32 in) to allow for the greater amount of wear now permissible (about 38 mm or 128,750 km, 1½ in or 80,000 miles). This remained standard until the late 1920s, when the development of high speed motors of smaller dimensions enabled 686 mm (27 in) wheels to be used. Spoked wheel-centres were usual, but mechanization of production later brought in the pressed disc wheel.

Re-wheeling a tram in the workshops of the Lincoln Corporation Tramways, about 1914.

Motors and Control

Traction Motors

At the turn of the century, tramway motors were of the four-pole totally-enclosed type without any forced ventilation, and a large motor had to be used to ensure that there was enough casing area to dissipate the heat generated. The next ten years saw the introduction of commutating poles or 'interpoles' and the introduction of self-ventilation by an armature-mounted fan that drew air through the armature and the field system. The use of 'interpoles' between the main poles to bridge the magnetically neutral regions reduced motor maintenance by minimizing flash-overs and virtually eliminating sparking at the brushes, and self-ventilation allowed an appreciable increase in the service rating of the motor for a given temperature rise. This development continued throughout the 1920s, permitting a lighter weight and smaller dimensions for the same output, and also permitting the use of the 686 mm (27 in) wheel. An incidental benefit was that it became possible to build covered-top tramcars low enough to pass under 4·6 m (15 ft) railway bridges. The introduction of ball and roller armature-bearings, about 1924, effected a further reduction in maintenance. New insulating materials and new production

processes also helped to give improved reliability, reduced maintenance, and greater power for the same weight; the cumulative effect was a four-fold increase in one-hour rating (and an eight-fold increase in continuous rating) during the forty years from 1890 to 1930. In more recent years, tramway motors have shared in the continuing improvements in the electric motor, such as the introduction of glass fibre insulation. German tramway-type motors with double-end drive were chosen for the Tyne & Wear Metro, and are manufactured by GEC Traction under a Siemens licence.

Power Control
The principle of tramcar control is graduated rheostatic acceleration control with the motors connected first in series to start the car without excessive current consumption, and then (with a 'shunt' transition) in parallel to sustain the normal running speed. This had already been established by 1893. A major improvement invented by Professor Elihu Thomson and first applied in 1897 was the adoption of 'magnetic blow-out' to reduce arcing in the controller when power was shut off. Magnetic blow-out enabled the drum controller to handle higher power outputs, but was again outpaced by later increases in power rating, and the 1923–5 period saw the introduction of controllers depending on cam-operated contactors instead of the traditional drum-and-fingers for the positions at which arcing was most severe; these were generally used only for cars with

Westinghouse Type T controller.

a total horsepower exceeding 120, below which figure the drum-type controller continued in use. In some cases, re-motored cars were fitted with a line contactor separate from the controller, which by providing a separate means of breaking a heavy current overcame the drum-type controller's main disadvantage.

Tramcar controllers were made in Britain (originally to American designs) by the Dick, Kerr works at Preston, the Westinghouse factory at Trafford Park, the Brush company at Loughborough, British Thomson-Houston (Rugby) and the General Electric Co. at Witton, Birmingham. Dick, Kerr later became English Electric, and Westinghouse became Metropolitan-Vickers. These names, in raised brass letters on the controller-tops, became familiar to generations of tram passengers as they joined or left the car by the rear platform. Each manufacturer used a different style of controller handle, and the expert can identify the maker of a tram's equipment by the shape of this handle, often visible in photographs. The accompanying page from the catalogue of a leading brass-founder (Gabriel & Co.) is reproduced as a reference, with type identification by Philip Groves.

Most British tramways did not go beyond the cam-contactor stage, but Liverpool, Leeds and Glasgow took the further step of adopting full contactor control on their modern bogie cars, using two low-voltage master controllers and a single set of electro-pneumatic contactors, fed from the same air-compressor as the brakes. This equipment had been devised for use in multiple-unit trains, in which the Ministry of Transport would not allow high-voltage jumper cables between the cars, but the only tramway-type line to run cars in multiple unit was the Swansea & Mumbles Railway; all other tramway applications were to single cars, and the multiple-unit possibilities were not used.

Contactor control equipment still gave noticeable 'steps' in acceleration, and a further stage was the type of control devised for the American PCC-car, in which a multi-notch rheostat is used, with a pilot motor fed from a battery to actuate up to ninety-nine small contactors arranged in a circle. The motorman can usually select a given rate of acceleration, after which acceleration is automatic. Similar features are embodied in the control of almost all modern electric trains, but there has been a trend towards using fewer notches to reduce the cost. The 1970s have seen the application to trams of thyristor control with direct current chopper regulators, which combine stepless control of the tractive and braking forces with an appreciable saving in power consumption,

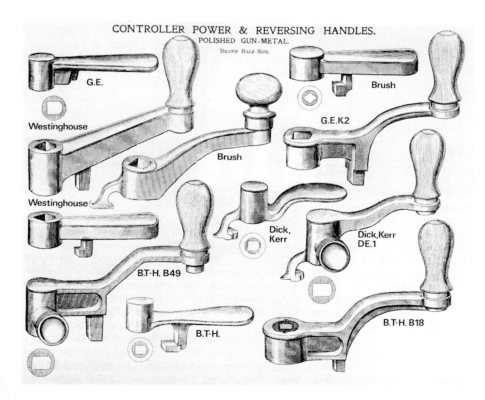

CONTROLLER POWER & REVERSING HANDLES.
POLISHED GUN-METAL.
DRAWN HALF SIZE.

G.E.

Brush

Westinghouse

G.E. K2

Brush

Westinghouse

Dick, Kerr

Dick, Kerr DE.1

B.T-H. B49

B.T-H.

B.T-H. B18

British Thomson-Houston B510 controller.

since there are no starting resistance losses. This form of control equipment is used in the newest Blackpool double-deck tram, No. 761.

Braking

Tramways in Britain were subject to regulations made by the Board of Trade or later by the Ministry of Transport, and the principal concern of their Inspecting Officers was the safety of the travelling public. These officers inspected every new tramway and fixed the maximum speeds, compulsory safety-stops, etc., and were particularly careful to ensure that every tram had adequate brakes. The tram's fine safety record shows how well they succeeded; for example, the trams at Southend-on-Sea ran for forty-one years and carried 510 million passengers without a single fatality.

Until about 1906, almost all British trams depended for normal service braking on a handbrake which applied cast-iron shoes to the rims of the wheels, a direct descendent of the horse car brake, but improved to obtain greater leverage, a greater braking force, and more rapid application. In addition, the car had an electric brake for use in emergency; in its earliest form this simply caused the two motors to generate into a short circuit, giving a very fierce braking effect, but this was later replaced by a graduated rheostatic brake in which electrical energy generated by the motors acting as dynamos would be fed to the starting resistances and dissipated into heat. This graduated rheostatic brake, applied by moving the controller handle anti-clockwise on to successive braking notches, was fitted to almost all cars built after 1900, though the earlier method was retained in some cases as an additional stand-by, especially in the form of an automatic run-back brake for routes with steep hills. The starting resistances, which were usually housed in a cabinet under the stairs, were originally of cast iron, which gradually gave way to steel after some cases of brake failure caused by fractured resistance-grids.

The rheostatic brake was not generally used in Britain for normal stops, lest it should overheat the resistances and overload the motors. Instead, as trams grew heavier, improvements were made to the handbrake; many towns adopted quick-acting geared handbrakes of the Ackley and Peacock types, and almost all adopted the ratchet handle, which could always be set at the most convenient position for working. With the later geared handbrakes, an effort of 41 kg (90 lb) applied to the handle would produce a tension in the brake-chain of almost 454 kg (1,000 lb), giving effective control of a car weighing from 12,000–15,000 kg (12 to 15 tons) without undue effort on the part of the motorman. The drawback was that the Board of Trade would not generally allow hand-braked trams to run at more than 26 km/h (16 mph), and the rule-books

A Southend-on-Sea tram driver; left hand on controller, right hand on brake-handle.

BRACE HANDLES, RATCHETS, SPRINGS.

No. 1337
Polished Gun Metal Brake Handle, with Revolving Horn Handle.
10½ in. centre ... 23/- each.
12 ,, ,, ... 24/- ,,
Drawn ⅛ full size.

No. 1331 2/10 each
Polished Brass Brake Spindle, Top Guide.
Drawn ⅛ full size.

No. 1338
Polished Gun Metal Brake Handle
10½ in. centre ... 21/6 each
12 ,, ,, ... 24/- ,,

No. 1339
Polished Gun Metal Brake Handle.
10½ in. centre ... 20/- each.
12 ,, ,, ... 21/- ,,

No. 574 5/6 each.
Polished Brass Brake Spindle, Top Guide,
Drawn ⅛ full size.

No. 1341
Polished Gun Metal Brake Handle.
10½ in. centre ... 22/- each
12 ,, ,, ... 23/6 ,,

No. 1333
Phosphor Bronze do. 5/- doz.
6/- ,,

No. 1336 13/- each.
Ratchet and Spindle Machined from Solid Steel, Hardened and Tempered. Complete with Cast-iron Nut

No. 1332 13/- each.
Ratchet and Spindle machined from Solid Steel, Hardened and Tempered.

No. 1335
Steel Ratchet Spring. 5/6 doz.
Phosphor Bronze do. 6/6 ,,

No. 1344 8/6 each
Ratchet and Spindle machined from Solid Steel, Hardened and Tempered.

No. 1334
Steel Ratchet Spring. 6/- doz.
Phosphor Bronze do. 7/- ,,

No. 1342 13/- each.
Ratchet and Spindle machined from Solid Steel, Hardened and Tempered.

No. 1340 13/- each.
Ratchet and Spindle machined from Solid Steel, Hardened and Tempered.

contained many local restrictions with lower speed limits. Despite this, the cars were rarely fitted with speedometers.

For higher speeds it was necessary to fit the cars with some form of power service braking. The London County Council tramways led the way by adopting and developing a magnetic track brake in which track-brake shoes were energized from the car motors acting as generators and were thereby attracted to the rails by magnetic force, this thrust also being transmitted by levers to the wheel brakes. Another arrangement was that adopted by Birmingham Corporation, in which the magnetic track brake operated through levers further track-brake shoes on the outer ends of the Burnley bogies. Other tramways adopted the magnetic track brake for emergency use, but when in the 1920s omnibus competition led to a desire to speed up tramway services in many provincial cities, this was more generally achieved by adopting an air-wheel brake.

An advantage which the tram has over any other road vehicle is its ability to use the rails for extra braking, and this principle was used on routes with steep hills. It took the form of a mechanical track brake, or slipper brake, and consisted of wooden or cast-iron blocks pressed on to the track by means of levers or screws operated from a second hand-

A Brill 22F bogie fitted with track-brake shoes.

wheel on the platform. It was simple and effective, and must have prevented scores of runaways in its time. In later years, cars using magnetic track brakes and running on hilly routes were required to have mechanical control of the magnetic track-brake shoes as if they were slippers, and in certain towns (including Birmingham and Bradford) the track shoes were applied by a strong spring and held off by the pressure of oil and compressed-air; this was known as the Spencer-Dawson air-oil brake after its inventors.

Lisbon has the world's steepest tramways.

Although high braking effects could be obtained by the use of magnetic braking, the post-1930 period in Britain saw a general change to air brakes, encouraged by the recommendations of the Ministry of Transport. In many cases a separate motorman's valve was fitted, but in some trams the control of air and magnetic brakes was combined in the Maley & Taunton Interlock, which prevented the air-wheel and air-track brakes from being applied at the same time and so lessening wheel adhesion. Turning the controller handle anti-clockwise to successive braking notches brought in first the air-wheel brake, then the air-track brake, then the magnetic track brake, and finally the magnetic track brake with automatic sanding. Large numbers of these equipments were used at Edinburgh, Glasgow, Dundee, Liverpool, Sheffield and elsewhere, and the system can still be seen today on British-equipped trams at Lisbon, which have to negotiate the world's steepest tramway gradients.

In recent years, tramways abroad have tended to change from air braking to all-electric braking, using dynamic brakes to bring the car almost to a stand and a battery-fed track brake to complete the stop and hold the car stationary. In Britain only one car was equipped in this way – Leeds City Transport 602 of 1953 – but the same equipment is used on the Tyne & Wear Metro. Regenerative braking, in which current is returned to the overhead line by the motors acting as dynamos, was tried from time to time but was rendered difficult in Britain by the compulsory division of the overhead line into relatively short sections isolated electrically from each other.

Current Collection

Trolley Heads and Wheels.

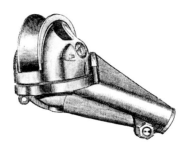

Trolley pole current collection; Grimsby, 1936.

Current Collection

By the turn of the century, it had been generally agreed that the best method of supplying current to trams was by an overhead trolley pole and wheel carried on a trolley standard. The sprung bow collector patented by Siemens was equally effective, but was limited at first to installations carried out by that company (the only British tramway example was at Sheerness). Most overhead-wire tramways used the swivelling-head trolley collector, others the fixed-head type usual in America.

If all our towns had permitted overhead wires in their streets, all would have been well, but some (including many London boroughs) considered these unsightly and required alternative systems which proved to be either more expensive or less reliable, or both. The London and Bournemouth tramways adopted the underground conduit system, with positive and negative conductor rails in a continuous conduit beneath the track; a 'plough' suspended from the car passed through a slot and made contact with the two conductor-rails. In Bournemouth the lines thus equipped were converted to the overhead

The London conduit system. Laying new tram track on Deptford Creek bridge, 1949.

A Wolverhampton Corporation tram running on the Lorain surface contact system, taking the current from skids between the rails. These studs were momentarily energized as the car passed over them.

A Siemens bow collector on a Preston-built tram at Gérardmer, France.

system in 1911, but the London system endured until July 1952, and is shown today by parts and track models in the London Transport Museum at Covent Garden.

Another method was the 'surface contact' system, which consisted of a series of metal studs along the centre line of the track which by means of electro-magnetic switches became 'live' during the passage of the car's magnetized contact-skate and 'dead' again afterwards. Apart from short-lived experiments six British tramways equipped lines on various surface-contact systems, but none was wholly successful, and each was sooner or later converted to the overhead trolley or underground conduit system. The system which provided the greatest degree of reliability was the Lorain installation at Wolverhampton. Surface-contact and conduit cars were often fitted with a trolley pole to allow through running over lines with overhead wires.

By 1928 overhead-wire tramways in many parts of Europe were using sliding current collectors (bow or pantograph) and both were then given a trial in Britain. Birmingham adopted the bow collector on certain routes, while the Swansea & Mumbles and Blackpool & Fleetwood cars were equipped with pantographs, though these were later discontinued at Blackpool because of problems encountered with

flying sand. In the next few years, Glasgow, Leeds, Dundee and Aberdeen adopted the Hungarian-designed Fischer bow collector, Sunderland (after also using bows) changed to pantographs, and Edinburgh, Gateshead and Grimsby & Immingham adopted the carbon-insert trolley skid, followed later by Bolton, Cardiff and Blackburn. All three sliding collectors normally used lubricated grooved-section wires in place of the earlier round-section wire. The carbon-insert skid was copied from trolleybus practice, but the bow and pantograph were both directly descended from the bow collector introduced in Germany by Siemens in 1889.

Blackpool tramways intend to change from trolley pole collection to Brecknell Willis single-arm pantographs. The picture shows the trial equipment of 1977 on tram No. 4.

Accessories

Lifeguards

Every electric tram used in Britain was fitted at each
end with an automatic lifeguard, a compulsory safety
device consisting of a vertical gate and a horizontal
tray, suspended a little way above the rails. On strik-
ing an obstruction, the gate would swing back and
cause the tray to drop and act as a scoop. This simple
device helps to explain the tramcar's excellent
safety record.

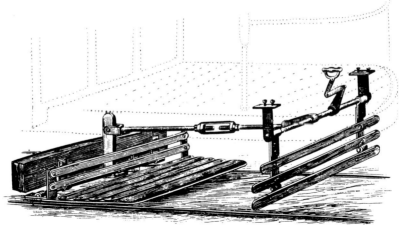

Headlamps

In early electric days, a few systems relied on the small lamp set in the bulkhead lantern panel. Generally, however, a large single lamp was fitted either in the centre of the dash panel or at canopy level. In early days, when the supply of electricity was often uncertain, oil was sometimes favoured as the illuminant. Modern trams generally have two headlamps set in the dash, instead of one, and also have stop-lights and flashing-light turning indicators.

Crowds boarding a Leicester tram at the Tramway Museum at Crich, Derbyshire.

Bells and Gongs

The usual means of warning other road users has always been a gong mounted under the platform and actuated by a pedal. The chime thus produced was the sound most readily associated with the British tramcar. In early years, a few operators had favoured a bell hung from the stair-rails, and in more recent times hooters or horns were employed on some cars. Communication between conductor and driver was usually by a pull-cord or rod-worked bell, but electric bells, worked by batteries, were also in use. From the 1920s, air-bells of the 'Numa' type, operated by air displacement, found much favour in Britain. Signals from the upper deck were often given by means of the conductor's whistle.

Drivers' Foot Gongs. (Above)

Conductors' Signal Bells.

Overhaul and Repair

On small tramways, the repair work was done in a portion of the car depot set aside for the purpose. Larger tramways had a separate repair and overhaul works, to which the cars would be taken every four to six months for inspection, re-turning of tyres, and smaller repairs, and about every two years for a general overhaul (in London, the police insisted that this be done every twelve months).

In an overhaul, the body was lifted clear of the trucks, which were then taken to the truck shop to have their motors disconnected, cleaned, and tested for insulation. The wheels were then re-turned or re-tyred according to the amount of wear, new tyres being fitted on to the wheel centres in a gas jet tyre-furnace and then water-cooled, forcing the tyre to shrink tightly on to the wheel centre, no other fastening being necessary. Motors were re-wound when necessary, and tested on 25 per cent overload for four or five hours before being replaced in the trucks. Meanwhile, the car bodies were inspected, renovated as necessary, the lights, wiring and switches tested for insulation, and seats repaired or replaced, the whole overhaul taking from four to seven days. The trucks and cars were then reassembled and taken into the paintshop for repainting and revarnishing, though the quality of the original paint was generally sufficient to last through several overhaul periods, being retouched and revarnished as necessary.

The Glasgow Corporation Tramways overhaul works at Coplawhill in 1958.

Illuminated Trams

In the heyday of municipal tramway operation in Britain, most large systems had a Decorated Car which could tour the town on civic and national occasions, decked out in a display of coloured lights. With the replacement of electric vehicles by motor buses this tradition has almost died out – except at Blackpool.

Blackpool's autumn Illuminations are world-famous. They extend the holiday season each year by several weeks, attracting more than two million people. Fairy lights are strung from the tramway standards along 11 km (7 miles) of Promenade, illuminated tableaux are put up in the gardens, piers, buildings and fountains are floodlit, and – best of all – the Transport Department brings out the finest-ever specimens of the Illuminated Tramcar. There are four of them at present – the Rocket (Tramnik One) of 1961, the Santa Fe Train (engine and car) of 1962, the Shell Hovertram of 1963, and the frigate HMS Blackpool of 1965. Earlier illuminated trams included the Lifeboat and the Gondola, and another one recently withdrawn was the Blackpool Belle, built in 1959 to represent a Mississippi river-steamer. The nine-week Illuminations season extends from the Thursday after the summer bank holiday until the last weekend in October.

A Blackpool illuminated tram of 1949.

Tramways in the British Isles

Blackpool Borough Transport,
Blundell Street, Blackpool FY1 5DD

Douglas Corporation horse tramway,
Strathallan Crescent, Douglas, Isle of Man

Great Orme Tramway,
Victoria Station, Church Walks,
Llandudno, Gwynedd

Manx Electric Railway,
Terminus Building,
Strathallan Crescent, Douglas, Isle of Man

Seaton and District Electric Tramway,
Harbour Road, Seaton, Devon EX12 2NQ

Snaefell Mountain Railway,
Laxey, Isle of Man

Volks Electric Railway,
Brighton, East Sussex

Pier tramways:
Hythe (Hants), Ramsey (Isle of Man)

Cliff tramways (funiculars):
Aberystwyth, Bournemouth, Bridgnorth,
Broadstairs, Douglas, Folkestone,
Hastings, Llechwedd Quarries, Lynton,
Saltburn, Scarborough, Southend, Torquay.

Tramway Museums to Visit

Belfast Transport Museum,
Witham Street, Newtownards Road, Belfast

Black Country Museum,
Tipton Road, Dudley, West Midlands DY1 4SQ
(tramway display under construction)

Bradford Industrial Museum,
Moorside Mills, Moorside Road,
Bradford BD2 3HP

Douglas cable car display at horse tram depot,
Strathallan Crescent, Douglas, Isle of Man

East Anglia Transport Museum,
Chapel Road, Carlton Colville, Lowestoft

Edinburgh Transport Museum,
Lothian Region Transport, Shrubhill
Depot, Leith Walk, Edinburgh
(visits by appointment)

Glasgow Museum of Transport,
25 Albert Drive, Glasgow G41 2PE

Hull Transport Museum,
36 High Street, Kingston upon Hull

London Transport Museum,
39 Wellington Street. London WC2E 7BB

Manchester Transport Museum Society,
Heaton Park Tramway, Manchester

Manx Electric Railway Museum,
Ramsey, Isle of Man

Museum of Science and Industry,
Newhall Street, Birmingham

North of England Open Air Museum,
Beamish Hall, Stanley, Co. Durham

Science Museum,
Exhibition Road, South Kensington,
London SW7 2DD

Steamport Transport Museum.
Derby Road Locomotive Depot,
Southport, Merseyside

The Tramway Museum,
Crich, Matlock, Derbyshire DE4 5DP

There is abundant literature on tramways. All tramway books currently in print may be inspected and purchased at the Tramway Museum bookshop at Crich, and the other museums generally stock those titles relating to their area or their exhibits. Postal sales are handled by the Tramway Museum and also by the Light Rail Transit Association, 13A The Precinct, Broxbourne, Herts EN10 7HY, joint publishers with Ian Allan Ltd. of the monthly magazine *Modern Tramway* and publishers of its historical counterpart *Tramway Review*. Readers wishing to build model trams can obtain information from the Tramway and Light Railway Society, 6 The Woodlands, Brightlingsea, Essex

No. 951   Badge.
Brass or Gun Metal   8/-
German Silver -   - 16/-

No. 950   Badge.
Brass or Gun Metal   8/-
German Silver -   - 16/-

Acknowledgments

The author and publisher would like to thank the following for their generous help in providing illustrations for this book.

Australian Information Service 113
Author 20, 27, 32, 37, 44, 73, 88, 94, 97, 102, 105, 106, 111, 112, 140
Author's Collection 24, 41, 42, 77, 124, 127, 130, 133, 139, 141, 148
C. Berry 34
P. H. Bonnet 103
C. E. Box 128
Brown Boveri 104
R. J. Buckley 114
J. D. Burton 45
W. A. Camwell 51
The late D. Conrad 64
R. Elliott 43, 65
'The Engineer' 23
Fox Photos 86
GEC Traction 71, 89, 136
The late W. Hallgarth 123, 134
J. B. Horne/LCPT 91
Hull Museums 16
J. Ibanez 108
A. A. Jackson 47
Kent County Library 54
Kohler, Bochum 107
J. Law 144
C. E. Lee 15, 25, 28, 30, 31, 33, 137
Leicestershire Record Office 63, 75, 92, 116
London Transport 83
Mather & Platt *frontispiece*
M. E. Mawson 96
R. W. Mercer 17
J. H. Meredith 109, 110
A. G. Merrells 138

Motherwell Library (Hurst Nelson Collection) 68, 72, 76, 79–81, 84, 101, 115, 117–9
G. S. Palmer 99
F. K. Pearson 36
H. B. Priestley 135
A. Ralphs 62
Sheffield Newspapers 6
R. Sims 60, 129
M. R. Taplin 132
C. Taylor 19
R. Temmerman 122
G. R. Thomas 87
Tramway Museum Society (R. B. Parr Collection) 35, 46, 48, 50, 53, 58, 59, 61, 66, 67, 120, 121, 125, 131
Triplex Ltd. 90
T. Walmsley 98
J. S. Webb 57
The late F. E. Wilson 21
R. L. Wilson 70
R. J. S. Wiseman 8, 95
W. J. Wyse 93
I. A. Yearsley 143

Fittings and accessories are reproduced from a pre-1914 catalogue of Gabriel & Co. Ltd., Birmingham, in the author's collection.

Index

152

Source Books

Aircraft
Armoured Fighting Vehicles
Commercial Vehicles
Dinghies
Hydrofoils and Hovercraft
Industrial Past
Locomotives
Military Support Vehicles
Motor Cars
Motorcycles
Naval Aircraft and Aircraft Carriers
Ships
Submarines and Submersibles
Tractors and Farm Machinery
Trams
Twentieth Century Warships
Underground Railways
Veteran Cars
Vintage and Post Vintage Cars
Windmills and Watermills
World War 1 Weapons and Uniforms
World War 2 Weapons and Uniforms